Shift-Clr/Home

I0009989

Shift-Clr/Home

SHIFT-CLR/HOME

More 8-bit Thoughts In A GigaBit World

by

Lenard R. Roach

SHIFT-CLR/HOME
More 8 bit Thoughts In A GigaBit World
Copyright and © 2019 by Lenard R. Roach
All rights reserved
Cover design copyright and © 2019 by Timothy Montee
All rights reserved
Printed in the United States of America

Table Of Contents

Introduction 7
Acknowledgments 9
Foresight Brings Hindsight To A Commodore Program 11
A View Of Commodore From Four Legs 19
Growing Pains 29
Growing Pains Part Deux (Problems With Check Mate) 37
Growing Pains Part Tres (TEA and TEA 4.2) 43
Growing Pains Part Quad (Continued Work On "The Ledger")...49
Growing Pains Part Fin   (Resurrection Of A Lost Program) 55
Growing Pains Part Six   (The Program That Never Was) 59
Growing Pains Part Siv   (Where I Learned To Code In Style) ... 65
Growing Pains Part Octo (Tying It All Together) 69
Programming In BASIC -- A Root Canal With No Anesthetic ... 73
Thanks For The Memory 81
Why I Use A Commodore 89
A Commodore Christmas 97
If Jesus Owned A Commodore 105
If Wisdom Wore Tennis Shoes 123
Let The Magic Begin Anew 129
Fruit Loops And Corn Dogs 139
The Commodore Jedi Master 147
What Else Can Be Said? 155
It Might Bear Repeating 161
Once And Future Commodore 167
In Search Of Specific Software 173
Programming Conundrums 179
The Time Is At Hand 187
And The Beat Goes On 195
Christmas Comes Early To The Roach Center 203
Commodore Therapy 211
Come Sit Right Back And You'll Hear A Tale 219

Shift-Clr/Home

6

Introduction

Greetings fellow retro user of all things Commodore!

The reprint of my first book, "Run/Stop-Restore" cleverly entitled "Run/Stop-Restore: 10th Anniversary Edition," has sold so well among the Commodore community, I was asked by a user or two to compile a sequel book of new scribblings coming from the pages of magazines like "Commodore Free" and "Reset" and newsletters like "Ryte Bytes" and "The Interface." What you hold in your hands now is the next installment in that series.

This volume is written in a similar style as its predecessors and I offer a similar form of comedy, inspiration, and a little knowledge. This book is more is more story and commentary than it will be practical education in BASIC.

One thing I have done is reduce the commentary that appeared at the front of each essay and wrote those commentaries for a group of essays. This should allow you, the reader, to get right into each chapter without having my word processor bog it down. For those who are curious, yes, this will be a similar cluster mess that took two interviews in "Commodore Free" to explain. Please be ready to ride a roller coaster of Commodore information and commentary that will make "Shift-Clr/Home" one of the most unique books about the Commodore you will ever read.

Even as this book goes to press, an as of yet untitled volume of more Commodore commentaries will be going through the writing and editing stage with hopes of a not too distant future release. So please, enjoy walking through the pages of "Shift-Clr/Home." Each essay in this book is easy to read and very short so you can finish a chapter before you have to get up from The Throne.

Shift-Clr/Home

Acknowledgments

Many men and women helped extensively into making this book a success. I'm only going to mention a few here; there's just too many of you...

TO THE EDITORS -- of "Commodore Free," "Reset," "The Interface," and "Ryte Bytes" for granting me Carte Blanche rights to reprint these essays, commentaries, and articles in this book and permission to copyright said material in my name. Without their permission, this book would not exist. Gracias, señors and señoras.

DON & ELLIE ZUEL (aka "Mom and Dad") -- Who love me as they would a son, making me an added addition to the Zuel clan and not treating as a "replacement" for their lost son, Carl, but gave me my own place at the dinner table. Though "orphaned" in 2004 by the passing of my natural mother, The Zuels made absolutely sure I still had a mom and dad in these future years. I love you.

WYNN ROACH -- My lovely and vivacious sister in law who took an entire file of gibberish sent as an attachment in an email and turned it into a well honed, fine piece of manuscript. I just wrote the words; she was able to make some sort of sense out of them. Thanks, sis. Love you.

TWO GENERATIONS OF ROACH BOYS -- That would be my egocentric brothers, Roger and Bruce; Roger's son, Anthony; Bruce's son, Christopher; and my own two "Supermen," Robert and Gabriel, all of whom would, if I didn't burn up a Commodore keyboard at least once a year, would hunt me down and kick my fanny, wanting to know why I was slacking. Thanks for the "motivation," guys. The next round of A&W is on me (but only one round.)

TAMMY LYNN ROACH -- Bruce's wife for just being as sweet as maple and corn syrup swirled with honey. She wouldn't give up on a dead dog, which was who she found banging his head on a Commodore desk thinking of something to write. Her constant gentle motivation brought this book to where it is now.

And ...

THE MEN AND WOMEN OF THE FRESNO COMMODORE USER GROUP – Who gave me a platform after the exit of the Commodore Users Group of Kansas City to express my Commodore ideas and comments. Thanks, team. We're number one! All others are number two or lower ....

TITLE: Foresight Brings Hindsight To A Commodore Program

POINT OF ORIGIN: Commodore Free Magazine

MODE: Essay

SYNOPSIS: Lenard gets into an emotional and logical description on the "how tos" of writing and running his program, "The Ledger."

Shift-Clr/Home

Foresight Brings Hindsight To A Commodore Program

Apologies to you, dear reader of Commodore Free, for my hiatus from writing in this august magazine that celebrates every month our fondness for our beloved machine. I could give one of a dozen excuses for my absence but all of them would be lame and senseless. Let's just say that it has been sheer lack of enthusiasm that has kept me from these digital pages, but I am thankful that our illustrious editor-in-chief and publisher Mr. Parker will still allow me to write for his magazine despite my absence. My thanks to him and to you all for your patience with this Mid-western U.S. redneck.

Ladies and gentlemen of Commodore, as you know times are hard all over the world. This recession which, I think, started with the housing market collapse in the United States and thus infected the finances of the rest of the world has all of us strapped; scraping to save whatever dollar, pound, or kugarant we have as we first as individuals, then as nations, try our best to scramble our wages around enough to make ends meet and keep ourselves from losing everything. Usually what we need to possibly do is just sit down with our families and take financial inventory of what we have coming in and, conversely, a list of what's going out. If you keep a careful grip on what's going where and when, it makes it better to know what is left and how to allocate same.

I've been pounding on my Commodore off and on for about 20 years now and have, in my own estimation (no ego problems here <G>), come up with some pretty good working models of money management software written entirely in BASIC for easy manipulation by those who have a working knowledge of the language. These ideas were birthed from an idea I got from a type-in program from "Run" magazine back in the day called "Money Manager with EZ Budget." Though "Money Manager" is a capable program to balance your checkbook and see how bills are paid each month, I figured in my own little redneck way that Rex Dey (the program's creator) needed an expansion on his idea. Thus was written by Yours Truly a little helper of a BASIC program who's working name is, "The Ledger."

"The Ledger" allows the user to record all the information about a debt, including how much is owed and when to pay it, then saves all that information in a one block sequential file on drive 8 of your computer. Each debt has its own file so there is little chance of mixing up the information by the constant swap of data that occurs sometimes with more complex programs. "The Ledger" allows you to make a payment on account and records that number in the same file as the information file.

I pulled this program out of the cobwebs of my forgotten Commodore software at the close of 2014 (the program is about a two years old) when I decided after several (and I mean *SEVERAL*) calls from a credit card company to my work phone demanding payment on the account that I already paid on. Having a lack of data on the account before me made it hard to prove telephonically that I made the payment and to give the proper information. My desk at home is strewn with bills and papers so locating information was hard. Then it struck me one night that I sat down at the Commodore and wrote a 27 block program that would allow me to electronically keep track of my bills and give proper information to anyone who contacted me by simply booting up my Commodore, loading the software, then calling up the "SEQ" file containing the information, and quoting from the monitor what I have done and when.

I found the disk containing "The Ledger" and loaded it from drive 8 into the Commodore's memory. My son was right back when he was 11 years old and suffering under leukemia treatments. I was working on a play for church one day and when I got writer's block he commented, "Dad, just walk away from it for a while and come back to it later with a fresh perspective." Well, being in "cold storage" for two years allowed me to see what I had to still do with "The Ledger," so immediately I started working on it again, adding new commands like a directory reader and an expanded menu selection. It took me a couple of weeks of late nights and several sheets of printer paper looking for misplaced semi-colons and strings to get "The Ledger" up to a better working order. Sure, the program was all right in its Version 1 style, but the extra added commands gave more control of the data to the user. It took me about two hours of data input to get my twelve debts (and counting) I have saved to one block "SEQ" files that can be read by "The Ledger," but I wasn't going to sit at the keyboard waiting for the credit card people to call; I immediately got onto the phone and started the interaction, but this time with "The Ledger" loaded in front of me, I could give the proper information as to how much I paid and to which office it was sent to. This shut the hose heads up and they just thanked me for my information, then hung up the phone.

When a user loads "The Ledger" for the first time, he or she is faced with the painstaking task of entering every bill into the program's database. Some of the questions asked by the File Creation subroutine may not have an answer that can be found on a statement, so I personally would type "none" or "not found" in that space to continue on. To make the program work the best, be sure to fill in every question asked by the File Creation subroutine with a word, number, or symbol. After all the data for a bill statement is entered, the program asks if you want to save the data and what name you want to save it under. Once a file name has been chosen, the program saves that data in the aforementioned one block data file.

What I find fun in the program is paying on a statement and entering that number in the "Make A Payment On Account" subroutine. Here in this part of the program a user just calls up the file to make a payment on. The program will then tell you how much you owe and how much of a payment is demanded to keep the account current with the party owed. You can opt to pay that amount or pay a different amount. I usually choose the "What Amount Then?" option for I personally pay weekly on as many bills as possible until the bills are all paid or I reduce the payment to a point where a paycheck will cover the debt. My weird method of debt paying is what I like to call "chopping down the tree;" each stroke of the pen on a check send a little to the party owed, making it small enough for one final check can pay it off. On some bills, this "chopping" process will take several months, if not a year or two; others will be paid in a couple of months and out of my life forever; reoccurring bills like mortgages and utilities get chopped down to their smallest level possible, then a final WHACK at the end of the month sends it falling and out of the way till the next cycle.

This brings me to the part of the program that I don't like to use, but it is a necessary evil when it comes to reoccurring debts, and that's the "Update Statement On Account" subroutine. Selecting this option from the main menu puts the user into a place where, when the file name is inputted, they have to make changes to the data like what the new payment is and when it is due. A single letter selection allows the user to save all this data again as new, and the file is updated.

One of the things about "The Ledger" that a person may not like is that the program only saves the current data inputted into the subroutines, thus eliminating, or "erasing" any previous information in favor of the new inputs. A simple fix to this apparent foupaugh is to save any new data as a separate file on the disk. For example, instead of selecting "Y" at the "Save Data As:" input, choose "N" and save the new data under a different file name. In my case with, say, the electric bill, I would save it as "ELECTRIC 1/15(1)," indicating that this bill is the electric bill for

January 2015, and the bracketed number shows that I'm making the first installment on the bill.

This program has helped me in my constant battle against creditors, collectors, and other hose heads that want to get into my wallet and take food money away from my family. I don't know how it is in the rest of the United States or the rest of the world, but sometimes a little money each week going to the accounts receivable department of a collector is better than not receiving anything at all. It is also fun to watch what I owe a business or service being calculated downward by the program's amount calculator so I know how much I owe and when.

Sadly, this program still needs a lot of work. I have demonstrated Version 1 at the Las Vegas CommVEx Commodore computer exposition a few years back, but the updates and additions have yet to be viewed by the Commodore public. The hard thing about alpha testing programs is that the programmer knows how to get around certain "quirks and bugs" in the work where a beta tester would find it a problem and not know what to do. My prayer for a general release date for "The Ledger" is July 31st, 2015, but beta testing should start sometime in late February or early March of that year. I will be looking for volunteers who have the time to run "The Ledger" through its paces and finding bugs that I don't know about and giving suggestions to make the program better. I know that most Commodore users have gone well past BASIC programming and are working in much more complex languages, and I am still a novice in the programming field, but any suggestions on making the program better would be beneficial.

If you are interested in becoming a beta tester for "The Ledger" or any future programs that come from The Roach Center For BASIC Commodore Studies, then please let your intent be known to me by either posting on my Facebook page (Lenard Roach), my website (www.lenardroach.com), or just blast me an email at lenardroach@yahoo.com. Your input could be exactly what takes "The Ledger" and other Commodore works from a good program to a great one.

TITLE: A View Of Commodore From Four Legs

POINT OF ORIGIN: Commodore Free Magazine

MODE: Essay

SYNOPSIS: Lenard, writing in the guise of one of his many puppet characters, describes the trip to and from The Commodore Las Vegas Exposition, as well as the show itself. This particular visit was in 2015.

Shift-Clr/Home

A View Of Commodore From Four Legs

-by Theodore J. Sheepdog

I am a dog, which goes without saying, but I am the lucky dog that got to go with a bunch of people from Kansas City to the 2015 Commodore Las Vegas show held in, where else, Las Vegas. I guess I should start at the beginning ...

I was asked by Lenard Roach one Sunday to go with him and his friends to the CommVEx. As a dog, it's hard to get my big paws onto a Commodore keyboard, but as a gamer dog I definitely enjoy using the Commodore, especially the 64 version, as a gaming source right along with my Xbox 360 and PS3. I enjoy all the classic games made for the Commodore 64 like "Ghostbusters" and "The Three Stooges" (these are my favorite C64 games) among others. I also learned that this trip was more than just a fun time, but Lenard wanted me to make a video of my visit so it can be shown at Glad Tidings church to the kids who enjoy my rantings and ravings every week or two in Sunday School class. I told Lenard that would be a great idea (especially since he was going to pick up all my expenses).

We left in a rented black and silver (Jedi colors) 2015 Chrysler Town and Country on Thursday July 16th at nine in the morning. We were suppose to leave a 6 am but the failure on not one, not two, but three alarm clocks to ring made for a late start to the show. Our first stop was to the small town of Keytesville, Missouri where Lenard's long time friend, web designer, photographer, and camera person The Vector lived. This was a 2 1/2 hour drive directly into middle north Missouri down two lane highways that only reached a maximum speed of 60 miles per hour. At noon we had The Vector and his gear loaded into the van and booked our way back to Kansas City. For some insane reason the on board GPS told us the quickest was to our next stop was back home. We explored other

21

options, like going through Sedalia, but Calibur, our main driver and Lenard's son, was already frustrated with two lane highways and wanted to hit some interstate and some 70 miles per hour for a change.

So, to Kansas City we returned, grabbing Interstate 35 to Olathe, then exiting onto US 169 south. This is a weird way to go, I thought, since our next stop, Tulsa, Oklahoma, was directly down Interstate 35, but Calibur set the GPS to avoid toll roads so here we were going down US 169 towards Tulsa, along with about a dozen or so semi tracker trailers who also wanted to avoid toll roads because, from what was explained to me, it costs about $100 per semi to travel the turnpike. This way expenses could be saved on the drivers.

At three o'clock in the afternoon we made it to stop number two where the son of the late and great Commodore guru, Carl Zuel, lived with his mom and sister. His name? Hunter Tiberius Zuel. Yes, just like in Star Trek. Lenard met with Hunter's mom and sister and made sure all goodbyes were exchanged before departing, at last, for Las Vegas. I thought we were going to see some of those purple mountain majesties like the American national anthem sings about when we passed through Colorado, but since we were so far south in the country, the GPS decided to take us through several US and state highways back to Interstate 35 just outside of Oklahoma City to connect with Interstate 40. Interstate 40 ran parallel to Route 66 that was made so famous in song, story, television, and motion pictures, but Interstate 40 went 70 miles per hour while Route 66 only went 60, and even that was sporadic. Calibur decided to run the way across the desert Southwest as the GPS directed.

After that things were a little hazy for the next eighteen to twenty hours since we basically stayed on Interstate 40 through Texas, New Mexico, and Arizona. Calibur didn't do all the driving;

everybody but Hunter and I took turns at the wheel, stopping multiple times for food, fuel, bathroom, drinks, and to let the Town and Country cool down. Temperatures in the desert reached as high as 105 to 110 degrees so when we did stop to fuel, Calibur would open the hood and check the radiator and oil to make sure they was plenty there. There's not much to talk about during this straight shot down Interstate 40. The van did come across a storm while crossing the Texas panhandle and for a while visibility was almost down to zero. All I did during most of that time was play on Calibur's Xbox 360 which he had hooked up to the monitor provided in the van that came down out of the ceiling. To get sound for the game console the driver and navigator had to surrender listening to the radio and allow the van stereo to be used for video sound. I also slept, ate, and went to the bathroom, but not all at once and not in the van. I have a little better training than that from obedience school.

By Friday afternoon we came across Interstate 15 which runs most of the length of Nevada and parts of Arizona. This highway took us directly into Las Vegas, where a slur of US, state, and interstate highways winded us around and through town until we came to 3500 Paradise Road, where resides the Mardi Gras Hotel and Casino. It was 2:45 in the afternoon Las Vegas time (we gained two hours from the trip by crossing into two time zones) and we just wanted to check in and get some sleep.

Already things were starting to get hairy and I don't mean my doggie fur; the hotel desk clerk informed us that each room required a $50 deposit before we could enter them. Lenard was furious. He only budgeted the trip for the monies intended for the journey there, food, and the way back; this was an unexpected expense that none of the team was prepared, but God was with us and each person came up with $50 (which had to be on a credit or debit card; no cash) and we clawed our way up to the third floor of the hotel (which looked more like a motel to me) and into our

rooms. Hunter and I were excited to be there since it was our first time to see Las Vegas. Right beside our hotel was the Las Vegas Monorail so we got to see it go by every once in a while.
Calibur and his friend Hatchi (who also came on the trip (sorry, I forgot to mention him)) immediately sacked out while Hunter, The Vector, Lenard, and I headed over to 1 Main Street to the Plaza Hotel and Casino where the CommVEx was being held with all of Lenard's Commodore equipment he brought for show and tell. Friday was the "Meet and Greet" for all of those who were going to attend the show and also set up day. I got to meet for the first time the event coordinator, Robert Bernardo, and was shown where Lenard was suppose to set up his equipment. Since Hunter never got to see a Commodore computer before, Lenard gave him the opportunity to set up the machine with all its drives and a monitor. Hunter and I were fascinated at how much cable and other little devices it took to make this simple single board computer run. It took Hunter 15 minutes with Lenard coaching to get the unit up and running, booted, and ready for the start of CommVEx 2015 the next day.

Saturday came. We started the show and the event coordinator had several drawings and door prizes to give away. Lenard did not have time to make a copy of his software to put as a give away and besides, Lenard said to me that his software was not ready for people to use. I was exempt from the drawings because, hey, I'm a dog. No harm, no foul to me; I was there for the games anyway. Most of the stuff talked about and shown at the CommVEx was way over my head, but I did make a few new friends there and that was the fun part. One guy, who's name escapes me at the moment, occupied the table behind Lenard and I. He was selling tons and tons of Commodore games at super reduced prices. I stuck my nose into the piles and piles of software and found games that I have never heard of for the Commodore computer like "1,000 Kung Fu Maniacs" and "Super Space Invaders" I enjoyed talking with the gentleman about different Commodore games and he even let me buy a couple. He was a big draw to the younger crowd, which was about three or four of us. Most of the Commodore users and programmers were well into their 40s, 50s, and early 60s.

One guy was there who's name does not bear repeating since he was such a pickle head to me and Lenard. The Vector, Lenard, and I explained to this individual that we were making a video of the show to broadcast on You Tube for the children back home. He didn't even look up at us and gave us an emphatic "NO!" When The Vector went around taking pictures of the show to put on Lenard's website, this son of an excrement eating cat started grilling The Vector about this like, "Why are you taking pictures?" and "Did you just take a photo of my program?" The Vector handled him with decor and demeanor but I wanted to bite him on the ankle and go to the bathroom on his Commodore. It's people like him that gives Commodore a bad name. For crying out sakes Commodore is a computer to enjoy not a thing to get all bent out of shape over. Sheesh! When it came to this person giving his presentation I didn't listen but took a short doggie nap under Lenard's table.

How did Lenard do on his presentation? Let's just say that he wasn't as prepared as he could have been. I've known Lenard to go on for a while about what he has done on the Commodore, but this, the one day out of the year to extol himself about the Commodore, and he blew it, not once but twice. During the whole weekend Lenard had a chance to make good on the Commodore and make some sales and he just let everything go to the wayside. He gave a lousy presentation and told some crummy jokes. It looks like Lenard saves his best humor for the kids back at church. I know this little embarrassment will be broadcasted over the Internet so be wary, viewer. It's not the best of Lenard Roach in Las Vegas so be ready for a disappointment.

The best presentations came from Commodore 128 creator Bil

Herd and the son of the late Jack Tramiel, Leonard Tramiel. Bil was hilarious when he told stories of his time at Commodore Business Machines and doing stuff like sleeping at the job and bashing a hole in the wall so he can get into his lab. Leonard spoke about his dad a little and some of the trues and falses in some of the latest Commodore history books that were just released. Bil talked with Lenard a little bit and during video time Bil made a video of me videoing him. He was fun. I hope to meet him again soon.

By Sunday afternoon towards evening the show came to an end. Names and phone numbers were exchanged by several attendees and a group photo of the club officers of the Fresno Commodore User Group was taken, of which Lenard was a part. Bil Herd was a part of the photos too and he and Lenard took a "gangsta" stance for the second shot. Let's face it; some people speak well but write horribly while others write well and speak horribly. Lenard is the latter, but he will have to start honing his speaking skills if he ever wants to go on book tours and share with all his adoring fans (I think he has three; I'm not sure). Well before the end of the show the team (that Lenard calls "The Roach Center For BASIC Commodore Studies") had the Town and Country loaded up with our gear and was waiting at the third level parking deck of the Plaza Hotel to take on the Hunter's Commodore equipment, Lenard's software, and The Vector's video collection, which was packed quickly. Down the ramp and a $2.00 parking bill later, we were on the road heading back to Kansas City, where again, the GPS took us through the desert Southwest to go first to Tulsa to drop off Hunter and his new/used Commodore 128 and respective gear. Again, not much to report except that the GPS was a little more accurate this time in getting us on east Interstate 40 to north Interstate 35. A detour off the interstate and onto north US 169 and we were at Hunter's abode, dropping off all of the Commodore 128 equipment and saying "goodbye." Hunter will look into his schedule to see if he will be attending CommVEx 2016.

The good thing about US 169 is that, even though its maximum speed limit was 65 miles per hour, it was a direct shot from Tulsa to Kansas City. Again, the GPS said to cut through our hometown to take The Vector back to Keytesville, but we weren't stupid and stopped by the RC4BCS HQ to drop off all of our clothes, gear, and equipment. This left only The Vector's suitcase and his video implements. I rode along because I would just be sitting at the center sleeping and being disturbed by Lenard's crazy cats.

The Vector treated us to dinner at a small diner in a little city in Missouri whose name I can't remember, but boy talk about food; burgers, ice cream, cake, malts, fries. I have to admit, I put on about a good five pounds just eating there because it was all good. It was here that The Vector's wife stopped in and picked The Vector up so we wouldn't have to drive all the way to Keytesville. After dinner Calibur, Hatchi, Lenard, and I headed back to Kansas City. The adventure came to an end at 10:00 pm on Monday, July 21st. We all dragged ourselves into the house and flopped into our appropriate beds.

I stayed the rest of the week at Lenard's while Calibur and Hatchi got the Town and Country ready for return to the rental place later that Tuesday afternoon. Lenard had to report to work at 5:30 am Tuesday at the convenience store while Calibur and Hatchi had the day off. Calibur reported to work Wednesday while Hatchi was smart enough to take the whole week off. I slept, played the occasional video game, and tried to get along with the cats.

There's not too much more to say about the trip except if you want to see the video The Vector made of me interviewing some of the attendees of CommVEx then go to https://youtu.be/4TY7aZeNjns. It was fun and I hope that this video goes viral soon.

Shift-Clr/Home

TITLE: Growing Pains

POINT OF ORIGIN: Commodore Free Magazine

MODE: Article series

SYNOPSIS: Lenard reviews his own Commodore creations and sees them from the knowledge and skills he has developed over the decades he has sat behind a Commodore keyboard. He offers suggestions on how he can improve said works and how it will make the mentioned programs better for the user. There are eight articles in the series.

Shift-Clr/Home

Growing Pains

Getting back from the 2015 Las Vegas CommVEx show put me in a humble mood. I realized that the Fat Guy here in Kansas City really shouldn't be jerking on the chains of productivity. I really need to sit down at the Commodore and start cranking out some programs like I said I would. I have high expectations but low initiative. This is a bad combination but it may be related to my mental condition; I'm not sure. What is sure is that there are 10 months left before the next Las Vegas meeting so I'd better hit the keyboard and start working on a few items that need to be tweaked or flat out re-done. However, before I get into the subject further I'd like to "detour into a cul-de-sac" as the pastor would say and ask for some assistance from you, the kind reader of my column...

I am looking all over the Internet and other sources for any and all construction sets that were made for the Commodore 64/128. I know it is highly likely that I can find all the Commodore construction sets online and available for easy download. Sadly, I run a "bear bonz" Commodore set up at the Roach Center For BASIC Commodore Studies so to simply "pull" such an item off the Internet is hard. I'm looking for the physical copy of these construction sets in good working order and I'll be glad to pay any reasonable price. If you have such a program in your collection (documentation included) and no longer have a use for it, then please consider selling it to me. Just send me a note to my website (www.lenardroach.com) with what you have and the price plus shipping. No reasonable offer will be refused. I'll even take duplicates of what I already got just to have backups. I want to thank each and every one of you in advance for your help.

Now to continue. Sitting down at my Commodore keyboard sometimes just isn't enough. I have five projects sitting in my Commodore disk file box that are in need of anything from minor code to complete re-works, and the biggest pain in my fat, flatulent, flabby fanny is my very first program I wrote for a magazine -- "Check It Out."

"Check It Out" would seem like a little waste of time to spend so much sweat on when with just a quick click of the mouse and your credit card handy you can pay mostly anything through the power of the Internet. However, I personally have some creditors that actually demand that I pay either by check, money order, or cashier's check; no credit or debit cards. So, I figure since I've got to sit down at a desk and physically write these companies a check, I might as well go whole hog and send everyone a check. "Check It Out" was born out of a need to write about thirty checks a month and at that time I was just beset with the wonderful condition of carpel tunnel syndrome. I wrote most of the code but the heart of the program (the subroutine that makes it all work) was a collaboration of myself and Commodore guru Carl Zuel. Carl's fifteen line subroutine he added makes the whole program worth it's while. I've tweaked and shuffled some of what he's done to "Check It Out" over several revisions of the work but I never destroyed the original function of that subroutine.

The funny thing about "Check It Out" is that it is never the same program for each dot matrix printer that it is used with it. In my naïveté at the time I thought that all dot matrix printers that were Commodore and Commodore compatible all followed the same program strings within their microprocessors. I was mistaken and should have seem this when I wrote a subsequent second program that would allow the program to work on the Commodore MPS 803. The final program that was published in RUN magazine was most compatible with the Commodore MPS 802, Commodore's business printer. It took several tries to get the PRINT#3 and empty spaces to make the program print all the information correctly on the front of a check. The program was not designed, but had to be, tweaked to work on the several models of Commodore and Commodore compatible printers that were available. I also never realized that some Commodore print commands were unrecognized by some of the compatible printers, the biggest of these commands being the PRINT#6 and the PRINT#10 commands.

After all these years and the long disappearance of my MPS 802 manual, I cannot remember what the PRINT#6 command did within the program, but I do know that it was working only with the MPS 802 and MPS 803 printers; any other printer that tried to access PRINT#6 would cause a "?" to be printed on the check. The PRINT#10 command caused the printer to go through a cold restart without turning the printer off then on. Again, printers that did not recognize the PRINT#10 command printed a "?" like it did on the PRINT#6 command.

Then there was the problem of spacing on the check. While PRINT#3 was a carriage return on the printer, causing the printer to move down to the next line, the empty PRINT commands (" ") moved the printer head from left to right, and, similar to PRINT#6 and PRINT#10, a misplaced space on the front of a check could mean the difference between acceptance or rejection by financial institutions trying to cash the check written using "Check It Out." That's was a big selling feature I pushed with the program was that everything fell into place and all a user of same would have to do is sign and mail the check.

The main controlling subroutine of "Check It Out" can be found in lines 900 to 1100. Here is where the print commands come in to play and the printer prints all the information written into all the inputs found in the first half of the program. Also, at the very beginning around lines 10 to 200 are some of the blank print strings used in adjusting the horizontal print on the check. These are the simplest factors to adjust by the addition or subtraction of any blank lines that will best make the dot matrix printer behave and locate everything accordingly. When it comes to adjusting the vertical print of the program one must (1) find out if PRINT#6 and PRINT#10 are recognized by the printer being used and (2) add or subtract PRINT#3 statements that best zeroes in on where each print line will start. The best results will occur when a check is inserted into the printer as flush to both the left side and the top of the printer head.

"Check It Out," in its 1992 published form, is nothing like what is sitting in my 5.25" file box here in Kansas City. With more miles on the keyboard under my belt I see some errors I've made in coding it. One was the location of my setup text before actual functions begin. In the original code, the stringed text was scattered throughout the program; updates have moved these "crunched" text lines to the beginning of the program. Also, I've inserted a new subroutine at around line 400 that gives the user an option to access any data written and saved using "Check Mate," which I hope to discuss in another article.

So far I've been batting 1.000 when it came to making my personal revisions of "Check It Out" to work on several dot matrix printers I have owned. The last success was getting the program to work was on a Star NX10-C. Now I possess a Star NX1000, which one would figure that being from the same family it would behave the same way....

Wrong!

This son of a bombastic mutant machine of a printer is nothing like its predecessor. I've been working on and off with this printer for about a year and this thing still beats me on trying to get "Check It Out" to work on it. Even some other programs that require a printer are having troubles obeying this printer. I'd hate to admit defeat because of one machine but I've almost run out of options. I've been given a creative mind so I'll pray and ponder over it some more before I order another printer.

I took this wonderful "mesterpiece" to show at CommVEx knowing perfectly well it wasn't ready for show or sale. Good thing for me is that I didn't show the program and worked instead with "The Ledger," which I also hope to discuss in another article.

Please learn from my mistakes and make sure your Commodore creation is perfectly ready for show and sale by alpha testing the living terror out of your project beforehand. Try to set up a circle of Commodore using friends who will be brutally candid with you about your work; such people hurt only to help you become better.

Shift-Clr/Home

Growing Pains Part Deux
(Problems With Check Mate)

I've been rummaging through some of the software that I have written over the past fifteen or so years comparing them to the knowledge that I have gained over the time and see where the problems lie in the program's construction and what can be done to fix it, if anything at all. This article will focus on the companion program to "Check It Out" called "Check Mate."

"Check Mate" was written under the influence of egomania as I had signed the contract with RUN Magazine over "Check It Out." Back in 1992 (when "Check It Out" made it's debut), I had this outrageous idea that I could sit on my fanny, in my underwear, and program on the Commodore all day and never have to see the inside of a factory or workplace ever again. My soon to be ex-wife just had our second son and I was thinking (at the time) that it would be great to sit at home, in the aforementioned attire, and be Mr. Mom and Mr. Commodore Programmer and she could go out and do woman things and never have to worry about money again. Whenever she would see me pounding on the Commodore she knew I was In the process of making money so we could eat, pay bills, and she could hang with her girlfriends during the day and we could, well, you know, at night. Little did I know that such a glamorous plan would change in the blink of an eye, or in this case, the flip of the calendar page.

It took me about one month to code "Check Mate" before I saw the first problem there would be with the program, and the problem wasn't with the program itself, but with its intended destination, which was to help with inputs to "Check It Out." As I looked over the work, I realized that I needed to make major improvements to "Check It Out" so what was written and saved to disk by "Check Mate" would cooperate with the code written in "Check It Out." Now how in blazes was I going to do this when "Check It Out" just went to press? This required a phone call to the offices of RUN Magazine in Arizona and speak to the HMIC (Head Man In Charge). Since I had the phone number close at hand, I quickly made the call. The phone rang and rang, but no answer came. I figured that everyone was out to lunch, at the same time. Yeah. That's it. I tried again several hours later, close to 5:00 pm Arizona time. Again the phone rang and rang, but no answer. Did they leave early on this day? To make a long story short I later found out that RUN Magazine had published its last issue and was no longer in business. "Check It Out" was placed in the very last issue of the magazine. Fine. I just got hosed by a bunch of Arizonians who gave not one indication of closing up shop. All my plans of being an at home Commodore programmer went up in smoke and down the drain all at the same time. I guess I'll have to get out the Sunday paper and peruse the Want Ads in search of that dreaded thing we Americans call, "a job."

Oh snap! What was I going to do with contacting anyone and letting them know that "Check It Out" was in need of revamping? I still sat on the original program, but I signed all the rights over to RUN in lieu of publication. If I allow anyone else, including myself, to release a re manufactured copy of "Check It Out" I would be in violation of United States Copyright laws. This little thing of copyright laws also affected "Check Mate" since "Check Mate" uses part of the coding for "Check It Out" to make "Check Mate" work. This was a real mess legally, but privately there was no problem. I could continue to make changes to "Check It Out" and develop "Check Mate" in the privacy of my own home, but when the work was done, what then? The legal blockade was still in place and would be in place for the next seventy five years after 1992, which would make it 2067. I would either be very dead at 103 or, if I live that long, I will be defecating and urinating on myself in some nursing home with no memory of who I am. What in God's good name was I going to do?

At the time, I told myself I wasn't going to worry about it. Seventy five years will give me more than enough time to work out all the problems with both programs, and hopefully I'll have time to spare to wrestle with this legal snafu. For now, let's make "Check It Out" and "Check Mate" the best BASIC programs written by a custodian that ever hit the Commodore universe. The first thing I had to look at was the set up of "Check Mate" itself.

When "Check Mate" was written I completely had in mind for it to be published by RUN magazine, so I kept the program within the parameters specified by that magazine. Their biggest concern was to make sure the programs published by the magazine were no more than twenty six blocks in length, which meant I had to do a lot of crunching in BASIC before I could send it. Also, the program lacked any sort of panache that would set it apart from other programs that it would share in the same pages. You don't mind selling the program to the publisher (or software developer) as long as you can see Joe Shmoe in the mall food court using your creation on his SX64. Because of the limitations, "Check Mate" lacked such fortitude. It was a plain, generic, database style program that would cooperate with "Check It Out."

As I sit back and look at this work over twenty years after I put the code into the Commodore 64, I realize that the whole program cannot stand alone; it must have "Check It Out" to work with, and, as I said before, "Check It Out" needed to be modified to accept the data created by "Check Mate" in order to work. The good thing about waiting all these years to open the program up again is that I have a carte blanche situation now, meaning I can do whatever I want to do to it without worries of breaking some publication's guidelines. The only person I have to impress right now is the man I see in the mirror every day at shaving time. Once it meets my specifications, I can release it to a select few for beta testing and ask them what I can do to improve the work. The one thing I like about programming is that nothing is ever set in concrete. A programmer can keep changing and modifying his creation, expanding it to its fullest potential, until the work has reached the pinnacle of perfection. The sad thing about programming is that, even when you think you've reached this pinnacle, some greasy haired, glasses wearing programming guru will take your work and expand it even more to cover areas that the original programmer never thought about. Such is the nature of the beast.

I'm not saying to anyone reading this that "Check Mate" is a piece of coding trash that should be erased from every Commodore disk still in existence; I'm saying that with a little love and thinking this program could make itself out to be a better work. I would like to add more color to the image of the opening screen and get more into detail on what options there are in the program and add some more options, if that will make it a better program. What I have to remember as I look at the code or run the program is that this program was never meant to be alone like "Check It Out," it is a helper to the same and will always be that way.

All in all, most of the work on "Check Mate" needs to be cosmetic and very little on structure and function. If any one has seen (or perhaps owns a copy of) my program "Obligator Coordinator" then they will know the extent to which I want to take "Check Mate" in the way of cosmetics. I want more color and a few more functions to make the program a little more practical. I piggy backed both "Check It Out" and "Check Mate" to load back and forth between each other. One thing I have to do when I go back in is to make sure all of the data strings are cleared out before another piece of information is inputted and clean up after the program has been used is thorough and complete.

When it comes to writing, be it coding or story telling, I hate the part of the job called the "editing mode." I want everything to flow and the piece to make an impression when either read or used the first time without any changes. This is fine for stories but try that stunt on a coding screen and you get a ton of "syntax errors" and "undefined statements" within the whole. The Commodore catches all the programming errors within itself when it does that, but it takes a good eye to see the errors in the printed page. I'd have to say that stories need to be beta tested just as much as programs do. Thankfully I have an actual editor in my family who can do this work for me without charge and I have beta testing for the world of Commodore to help make programming mistakes disappear.

In conclusion, I would like to say that when it comes to function, "Check Mate" makes the grade for which it was originally designed. When I get into it I will do little to it except what I have aforementioned in this article, but with all the programs I write, I would like to add a small, on screen documentation that will give overall use and tips on how to maximize the use of the program as seen from the eyes of the programmer. As always, I'd like to say that programming on the Commodore is both fun, nerve racking, and refreshing. I await, sometimes with anticipation, on the next idea that comes to mind for the Commodore.

Shift-Clr/Home

Growing Pains Part Tres
("The Envelope Addressor" (TEA) v1 and v4.2)

As I sat down in the genuine fake leather chair behind the keyboard of my stock Commodore 128, the screen was already displaying the main menu screen to my greatest Commodore BASIC program to date: That of what has come to be known as "The Envelope Addressor" v4.2, or it's better known acronym, "TEA 4.2". As I looked at the display, I leaned back in the chair with my hand on my chin, and asked myself, "How can I make this program better?"

If I remember my Sherlock Holmes correctly, the best thing to do when considering a course for the future is to seek counsel from the past, so I guess it would be best to start where "The Envelope Addressor" came from...

I was sitting at my desk one Sunday afternoon going over the bills for another month. My previous successful program, "Check It Out" was already loaded into my Commodore 128 (in 64 mode) and printing checks as I called them off. I won the battle with the pain of writing dozens of checks a month by hand, but the task of putting the return and recipient address onto the envelopes still remained. The selfish reason for coding "Check It Out" was my blasted carpel tunnel that set in over the years. It was getting too painful (and sometimes numbing) for me to wrestle with pen and ink over checks. With "Check It Out" the problem was solved, but new revelation revealed only half the problem was solved. Now I have to deal with the same recurring pain and numbness addressing envelopes as I did when I was writing checks. I looked at my (then) Star NX10-C printer with a freshly drafted check sitting in the rollers and said to myself, "If I did it before, I can do it again." So, that very evening I started drafting the source code for what, in the next three months would become, "The Envelope Addressor" v1.

The program ran similar to "Check It Out" in format; the program would guide you around your envelope allowing the user to put in the "To" and "From" addresses, but as a bonus, the program saved your input data to a small, compact, one block sequential file before going to print. My wrists were saved and my pain almost a memory. On a whim, I contacted Mr. Moorman of the "Loadstar" Commodore disk/magazine fame and inquired him in an email if he would be interested in seeing the work. He politely agreed so I sent him a image copy of the work, and I waited.

Two or three weeks went by before I nervously attempted to contact Mr. Moorman on how my program fared under his scrutiny. The next day he sent me a .d81 image copy of the latest issue of "Loadstar" with "The Envelope Addressor" neatly tucked into the digital pages along with his personal comments about the work, but not comments on the program, per se, but on it's structuring. Mr. Moorman stated that it has been a long time since he has seen a Commodore BASIC program so well uniformed that "The Envelope Addressor" was worth the "stopping of the presses" as it were, and fitting the program into the latest issue of "Loadstar". He went on to say that usually he encrypts all the programs published in "Loadstar" to deter piracy, but "The Envelope Addressor" was such a well structured program that he left its code unencrypted in the final print of the disk-zene so future contributors to "Loadstar" could see how a Commodore BASIC program should be presented. Score! I think ....

Then came the acid test, or as I liked to think of it as the "jack" acid test, and that test came from the noble, wise, and venerable men and women of the Commodore Users Group of Kansas City (Missouri). When they viewed the program from the disk they got from "Loadstar," they had some suggestions. They didn't want to change the code; they had some ideas to make the program more practical. A few examples were: Make the program print on smaller envelopes, like the smaller size #7 style. Get rid of the

"Attn:" format. That's good for businesses but most Commodore users nowadays are more home users; they won't need that feature. What about window style? Can you code a feature for those style of envelopes? Our resident United States post office worker suggested that, since Mexico is starting to adopt US Postal styles like zip codes, a "Country Designation" feature should be printable on the face of the envelope. Despite the ego boost given to me by the editor and publisher of "Loadstar," my wise Commodore comrades pulled my head out of the stratosphere and placed me again on good ol' terra firma. At first I was hurt by their criticism, but the more I used "The Envelope Addressor," the more I knew they were right -- again. So, two years later, on another Sunday evening after paying bills using "Check It Out" and "The Envelope Addressor," I listed the program text to view on my Commodore 1902 monitor screen and started tinkering around with the source code.

When I started working again with the code as a programmer instead of being an end user, I saw my Commodore friends were being too nice to me; there were a lot of things I could do to make "The Envelope Addressor" and much more handy and viable tool in the hands of the "every month" accounts payable person. Taking their suggestions, and a few of my own that I thought of, in the span of another two months I all but completely re-coded "The Envelope Addressor" into a Frankenstein model of its former self. I added an extended main menu; I re-coded the directory to allow the user to see which file was the "From" address (F/) and which was the "To" address (T/); I expanded the print lines to include #10 size envelopes, #7 size envelopes, single window envelopes, and double window (paycheck style) envelopes; I coded more sub menus with easy "back out to the main menu" access in case a user got lost in the maze of menus and sub menus; I did a lot of upgrading to it, so much so that "The Envelope Addressor" was no longer the same; similar, yes, but not the same.

A remodeled program needed a remodeled name. Nothing totally off the beaten path, but something that said, "I'm back and I'm buffed! Fear me!" Throughout the household of Roach, the program was jokingly called "TEA", so the family came up with "Tea For Two", which I translated into Commodore-eze as "TEA 4 2," which later transcribed into its final version, "TEA v4.2." With that little conundrum settled, and the re-coded program in place, it was a matter of redrawing an opening graphics boot screen, putting it in place on the master disk, and viola! Another Commodore masterpiece wrapped in the bacon of BASIC. Oh, before I forget, the graphics screen I drew was of two steaming cups of hot tea in heart and diamond studded tea cups, which really looked more like coffee mugs. I used the "Screen Gem" med-res graphics illustration program written by Mr. Godfrey many moons ago when the Ivory BBS package was the big thing in the United States.

One thing about both "TEA" and "TEA v4.2" was that they were the only programs I coded that I actually wrote documentation for. It was my first attempt to write "on screen" text, so I used hundreds of Print Statements, followed every several lines by a short subroutine which allowed the reader to "flip" back and forth among "pages." Two pages of handwritten text became twenty pages of "on screen" text. Since direct BASIC Print Statements do not word wrap, I had to physically space out the words so that the text would look uniformed on screen. That was tedious, long, boring, and mind numbing, but it did make for a great visual presentation on the Commodore monitor.

So, what happened to "TEA v4.2?" Lightning struck twice as I sent the new version of "The Envelope Addressor" to Mr. Moorman of "Loadstar" and he published it in a disk/magazine as well. "Loadstar" headquarters was hit by a tornado not too far from the close of the first decade of the 21st century and never recovered. Another great Commodore publication hit the dirt.

With all that out in the open we go back to the question that started this article: What can be done to make "TEA v4.2" a better program? With magazines like "Commodore Free" in publication and Commodore users coming together from all over the globe under its banner, I think making "TEA v4.2" more universally usable. I know in it's present form, the program can be used in the United States and Canada, but what about European or Eastern countries? How are their postal codes formatted? A project worth possibly perusing.

Also, I would like to make "TEA v4.2" work with the click of the Commodore mouse or tap of a Commodore joystick. Commodore has written a BASIC program in the appendix of "The Commodore 1351 Mouse Users Guide," and it works well, but, how do you make the mouse highlight what the arrow lands on and how do you make it understand that where the pointer is is what you want to access?

You use the left mouse button to access the desired field.

How do you make the program understand the clicking of the mouse button?

It's the same code as the using of the fire button on a joystick.

AND WHAT CODE IS THAT? SON OF A CUSSING CUSS WORD, I'VE HAD IT! I'm going to play "The Three Stooges" or something! At least there I have a reason to deal with silliness!

Shift-Clr/Home

Growing Pains Part Quad
(Continued Work On "The Ledger")

In this article I plan to go in depth on the youngest program in my entourage called "The Ledger." It is one of my favorites to date and is a "good friend" to me when I sit down to work on paying bills.

The idea of this program actually came from my ex-wife's method of how to pay the bills and track how much is owed in order to pay the debt off. I sat down with her ledger book and tried to transpose the data and columns from it into a working program for the Commodore 64. Oh yes, many bookkeeping programs already exist but I wanted one that actually emulated her style. My first attempt to create the ledger was called "Obligator Coordinator," which I took the time and the $25 dollars to copyright with the US Copyright Office in Washington, DC. I was really hoping to make a name for myself in the computer programming industry, but, as usual, my problem was marketing, and, with many computer users heading their way to PCs, a call for Commodore software was fading off into the sunset at the time. Usually when I code into existence a piece of software, I believe it the most pimping thing ever to hit the Commodore market -- heck, why not the entire computer universe! Once word hits the boards of my amazing program, users from all over the world will be blowing up my landline and stuffing my mailbox with orders! All I had to do was copy and mail. I would be making so many deposits at the bank that the tellers would not only know me by my first name but also start complaining that they had to deal with adding up all the checks I brought in. I didn't have high aspirations, I didn't have an inflated ego, I was a realist, knowing that this would *really* happen. When not even a curse word came back to me in any form of communications that the 1990s had to offer, I curled up into a fetal position and cried.

After months of musing I sat down at my Commodore 64 with "Obligator Coordinator" loaded into memory and started to use it myself. After a few minutes of inputting data there came the dreaded line no programmer wants to see in their work: SYNTAX ERROR IN .... What the? I ran this program through with the finest of toothed combs I could before I sent it to the copyright office. I found the offending line and made a quick repair. Running it again, "Obligator Coordinator" made it through the hump but a few minutes later another evil message appeared: TYPE MISMATCH ERROR IN ... I did what was natural, I called my Commodore every four and five letter curse words I could think of and even made up a couple for good measure. My Commodore just sat there not giving a care of how I felt or what I called it; the error message was still there on my screen. I banged my head on the computer desk wanting to know why. On the 17th whack an amazing thought came to me: Did I realize that the Great Omnipotent Grand Exalted Poobah Of The Universe And Other Surrounding Postal Codes just saved my fat, flatulent, flabby fanny from a fate worse than poverty? By not allowing a single sale of "Obligator Coordinator" I was spared the shame and humility of selling a defective product to the world at large, and undertaking the task of either refunding monies gathered or giving upgraded copies for free which would cost me more time and money in envelopes and postage. I took a big deep breath at the thought of this revelation and quickly gave thanks for being spared this personal tragedy brought on by my ego, and, with the program in my computer, I started making repairs.

But I'm giving away too much information that would be best kept for a future issue of "Commodore Free," but there is a lot of history behind the development of "The Ledger" that, without it, this commentary may not make much sense -- like it makes any sense now. Let's just say that "The Ledger" is a third attempt at trying to make a viable working Commodore program out of a paper system that worked well for years in the Roach household. The other two attempts were the aforementioned "Obligator Coordinator" and "Bill Attack!", both of which will be discussed in the future.

At first glance, "The Ledger" is the most comprehensive work I have done so far on making my ex-wife's paperwork into a Commodore reality, but one thing I wanted to do was make the program more "push button" friendly. The hardest part of using the program is inputting all the data off your bill statement into the Commodore and saving all that information under its own file name. This I don't think I can change much. There is a lot of data required for the files that little, or even nothing, to do with making the program work, but it is a great database to hold information for references.

When I looked at "The Ledger" after all this time (I think my last update was two years ago) I'm thinking that a time stamp would be helpful for future notes. The time stamp could also be used to roll over the next payment as a future reference. For example, the program could make note that you just made a house payment on 05/22/16 and your next payment won't be due until 06/22/16. This should be able to be done by assigning the month as a separate variable (like M) and then telling the Commodore that we are going to advance the M variable to the next month by using the formula: M=M+1. Then, when all the data is to where the user likes it, just press something like F1 and voila! The data is saved in a simple sequential file onto disk. Right now as it stands, "The Ledger" allows the user something like that, but it's the user that inputs that information in each and every time. This would almost eliminate that need.

Also, looking at it, I think a "blow up" of each bill would be a helpful addendum to the lines of BASIC that make "The Ledger" a useful tool. I already have something similar already in place but I want something more extravagant; more detailed. I'm thinking the page would run something like:

YOU OWE (total) ON THIS BILL.
THE MINIMUM PAYMENT OF (amount) IS DUE ON (date).
DO YOU WANT TO PAY (amount)? Y/N.

The user will be given the choice to pay a different amount and apply it to the debt. After the payment is posted in the Commodore the computer will announce:

A PAYMENT OF (amount) WAS POSTED ON (date).
YOUR BALANCE IS NOW (new total) WHICH WILL BE DUE ON (new date).
DO YOU WISH TO SAVE THIS DATA TO (file name)? Y/N.

If the user pays off the debt and the balance is zero, the Commodore can post a message on the screen that says something like:

CONGRATULATIONS! YOU'VE PAID OFF THESE SONS OF BELIAL! REWARD YOURSELF WITH A DOUBLE CHEESEBURGER FROM THE LOCAL SCARF N' BARF.

That might be a little extreme but you get the idea. Just to add humor I may add a micro word processor so the user can create a small 40 to 80 character congratulatory message and I add an RND(0) calculator so the Commodore can display up to, say, six messages that the user can do to celebrate each debt being paid off.

Of course, on reoccurring debts like utility and cellphone bills I will keep the "Change Data On Account" subroutine so the user can add the new totals into the database and start the nightmare all over again.

As you can read, "The Ledger" is already formidable as it is and does the job quite well in its present state, but, like I stated, the work could use some incredible cosmetic surgery and add some features to make it more user friendly and quicker to access and manipulate data. With this program being "the baby" of my Commodore works, I'm looking forward to sitting down at the Commodore and helping this baby grow into a beautiful, flourishing piece of the Commodore family.

Shift-Clr/Home

Growing Pains Part Fin
(Resurrection Of A Lost Program)

I was nosing around in my disk files just to see what kind of things I thought were necessary to hang on to. For somebody who doesn't play too many games I sure did have a lot of games on disk that I put into storage. I went through my two files of 5 1/4" disks and found that I would like to still hang onto these disks for some insane reason. I especially had a lot of music programs and I needed to take time to learn how to make music on my Commodore so I could have some of my favorite tunes produced by the SID chip and not everyone else's.

Onto the one and only file box I had containing 3 1/2" disks. I'm not a big fan of these disks since I can load five of the 5 1/4s" full of my ravings and rantings compared to only one 3 1/2". The 5 1/4s make me look more like a Commodore big shot than the 3 1/2s do, but I did condense a lot of my favorite type in games onto the smaller disks for room's sake.

I started to rifle through this box when, about midway in, I stumbled across a disk I labeled with an ink pen, "Roachware Vol. 1." I remember this disk from way back in 2000 when I took all the programming and word processing I did and filed it onto one disk, with subsequent disks to follow as I progressed into the 21st century. Volume 1 was where I stopped because life, as usual, got in the way of progress.

"Yeah, I'll boot this," I said to Hennessy the Commodore Cat, who was lying on the table above my 128, "and we'll see what I thought was important." Hennessy just shifted his head from his left paw to his right and went back to sleep, indicating his famous, "Whatever" feline attitude.

I booted the 128, loaded the intended disk into my favorite drive, the Commodore 1581, and loaded the disk's directory. A quick flash of the word READY and the input of LIST, then the tap of the RETURN key and history of my world from 2000 to about 2008 flashed before me in lines of sixteen characters or less. Basically, the disk contained many of my writings for church ministry that I won't get into in this article, but one particular program file did catch my attention. It was only called BILL8. Who did I know as Bill, why would I write a file about him, and why did I revise it about eight times? The only way to find out is to LOAD the program into memory and see what happens...

The monitor showed me that BILL8 is in reality a long abandoned program called "Bill Attack!" Since I didn't date the work I have no idea when I started or stopped working on it, but my best guess on dating this work would be about 1993 or 94, when I was trying to make a living from magazine publications. I really thought I reached the summit of my life back then: beautiful wife, two sons, a great job, and what I wanted; a writing career. It all crashed in a month when all things Commodore in the US went belly up. More on that at another time...

"Bill Attack" was a simple menu driven program coded in Commodore BASIC that was more of a note making program totally focused on word processing and little else to deal with paying bills. After all the inputs are satisfied, the program saves the data in a one block sequential file on a disk. If I remember right, I needed a program to keep up with all the bill collectors were telling me instead of trying to keep all their hogwash straight in my head. I've later learned that you should know that a bill collector is lying when their lips are moving and you need documented evidence of what was said. "Bill Attack" allowed a user to keep notes on what was said. I usually would use such things as who I talked to and at what time. Now what am I going to do with it?

A quick solution would be the following BASIC command line:

OPEN15,8,15:PRINT#15,"S0:BILL8":CLOSE15.

That would solve almost everything. "Obligator Coordinator" is an upgraded variant of "Bill Attack" so "Bill Attack" is not really necessary, except for the fact that it belongs in the Roach Anthology of Programs. But, if this program was worth it, what would I do to it to make it marketable to the Commodore public?

Apparently when I left off I was just starting to give the screen display some flair by adding a little color, but all I did was some white and a light red and nothing else. The red bled into the rest of the display making things look like somebody smeared a watermelon onto the monitor. Not attractive. I tried using the program by entering some random data to see the display on the input screens. I was impressed by how well each input took the place of the former input by overlapping. Sadly, when I went to save my bogus information the Commodore disk drive failed due to a simple (,8) telling the machine to save only to drive 8 and I was using drive 9 at the time, so I don't know how it fully functioned. I'm thinking of adding a drive access number to all my programs I'm reviewing in this series so the user can choose which drive to put data on. I've always liked that feature in works like GEOS and I'm thinking, "Why not?" I'll see how that may improve the working of the software.

I think I've mentioned this before, but programming in Commodore is like writing a symphony. Each tap on the keyboard brings harmony to the work as a whole and, when it is finished and the programmer types that fatal RUN command, the combination of key taps and algorithms begin to play together into a working conglomerate. Maybe the Rabbi Paul said it best in 1 Corinthians 12, "The body has many parts, but it is all one body." So, likewise, a program has many keystrokes, but it is all one program. Like

Colonel Hannibal Smith says in the "A-Team" series, "I love it when a plan comes together." I feel the same way when I program. So this little hidden blip in my program repertoire brings back where I really was when I started to take programming seriously.

I guess there's not much to do with a program code that you had planned on destroying anyway, but I have learned to give credit where credit is due and "Bill Attack" gave me a burst of expanding ideas to make two more prototypes that brought me to where I am now. Like my writing teacher always said, "Save everything; you never know, that napkin note may be your next best seller."

Growing Pains Part Six
(The Program That Never Was)

If I understand my agriculture correctly, when planting a seed you first dig a hole in the ground and bury it, then water and sunlight are added. In a few weeks a startling metamorphosis occurs as the apparently dead and buried seed cracks open and out of the cracked seed comes new life. Very soon the new life conquers any vestige of the seed until all that can be seen is the new life. Such was the work in coding the program "Obligator Coordinator." It was also a work of Commodore vengeance. Let me start from the beginning ...

"Obligator Coordinator" was a work of anger and ego. If anyone has read my book, "Run/Stop-Restore: 10th Anniversary Edition," then you read about the combat over copyright control of my work, "Check It Out." Basically, the people who bought all the software rights from the defunct "Run" magazine now owned it and I wanted to publish upgrades I made to the code. The new owners said that they would not release the rights of "Check It Out" to me without a monetary fee. I coded the cussing thing; I should have some rights! No. According to the "work for hire" contract I (hastily) signed, I surrendered *all* rights to the program in exchange for money. This also means that any upgrades I code for the program become the immediate and undisputed rights of the contract holder. This includes "Check Mate," which is a derivative of the code I wrote for "Check It Out." Expletive! There were two choices at this point: Drop my 5 1/4" disk of work on "Check Mate" and "Check It Out" upgrades into the shredder or file it away never to be seen by another human eye. I chose the latter.

This was not going to stop here, oh no! I'm going to sit down at my Commodore and code an awesome piece of software so fantastic that it will make my last two projects look like the handiwork of kindergartners! I crossed the house to the computer room, sat down at the Commodore, thrusted a blank 5 1/4" disk into the 1541-II disk drive, booted the system, poised my fingers on the keyboard, and ... banged my head on the computer desk with a wood cracking thunk. What was I thinking? "Check It Out" and "Checkmate" *were* my greatest Commodore achievements! Who was I fooling?

I leaned back in my computer chair and stared at the Commodore home screen and flashing cursor. Dover, my yellow striped tabby cat, came into the room and rubbed her head on my dangling right hand. I looked down while at the same time she looked up. She mewed. I scratched her head. I watched her as she walked over to the open cubby built into the computer desk where I store all my 5 1/4" disk files. She stood on her hind legs with her front paws supporting her on the ledge of the open cubby. A crouch, and a leap, and she was in the cubby, but there was no room for her and the two disk files so when she laid down in the cubby, all four of her feet pushed both files out of the cubby and onto the floor, where the files cracked open and about forty 5 1/4" disks spilled onto the computer room carpet. I looked at the mess, then looked into the cubby. Dover licked her right front paw, stretched out, and got comfortable.

This is an amazing thing about cats: They can destroy your entire living room, put it all in a pile right in the middle, climb to the top of said pile, lay down on top of said pile, look you square in the face with a look that says, "I didn't do a thing." Dogs: They make one piddle mark the size of a pence on your carpet and they *know* they have committed the greatest sacrilege. The dog looks at you with that face that says, "Oh snap! He's gonna kill me now!" Nonetheless, that stupid cat was not going to help me pick up those disks, so I got out of my chair and started picking up.

About half way into clean up I came across a disk label that caught my eye. "Bill Attack Work Disk" it read. What was this? It had my handwriting on it so it was something important. I sat back down, popped the blank out of the 1541-II, inserted the "Bill Attack Work Disk," and loaded the directory. The monitor showed me several different versions of this program, so I booted the latest version on the disk (I think it was "8") and waited. Very quickly I saw a data base style program used for mainly recording information and storing that information onto disk. I didn't see where the "attack" part of the program was; it was more like a coordinator than anything else. I exited the program and listed the code. Hmm. All this needs is a little subroutine here and a couple of GOTOs and GOSUBs there and this could be a viable work, but that name "Bill Attack" has got to go. I'll worry about that later...

It took me a couple of months of working about a hour a day on the program to get it to where I wanted it, but it still needed a name; one that would describe what the program did and still make it sound cool in just a couple of words. I remembered that I once called this work a "coordinator" but what can I put in front of that word to help make an impact? Bill Coordinator? No, that lacked pizzazz. How about "Obligator Coordinator?" It tells what the program does and it even rhymes. I'll stick with that.

Now to provide a little present for hose head publishers who scam off of hard working coders. I got onto the PC and pulled down a copy of Form TX from The United States Copyrights Office in Washington DC and printed same. But this form was for a book and I needed to copyright a program. What do I do? I searched my local library's website under "copyright forms" and I found the book, "Legal Care For Your Software" by (name). I went to my library and checked it out. I read it not once but twice and decided that this was too valuable of a resource not to have, so I ordered a copy from my local bookseller ($30) and read it again (my new copy had updates and new forms added). I filled out the TX Form and mailed it, a copy of the program text, and a $25 check to Washington. Six weeks later I had a bonafide Ownership Of

Copyright paper in my hands. Eat that you spastic, lard fanny, pickled headed, simpletons of the magazine industry! You're going to have to deal with *me* now instead of the other way around! I win ... or did I?

It was 1994. "Run" magazine was out of print for two years. "Commodore World," a magazine division of CMD Industries had just launched and wasn't willing to deal with me unless I "surrender all rights" to the software. At the time I was too much of an egocentric knucklehead to be dealt with, so "Obligator Coordinator" sat in my files never to be released. In about 2002 I heard about Mr. Moorman and "Loadstar" disk magazine and was about to contact him via the Internet and pitch "Obligator Coordinator" to him, but first I'd should boot a copy and see how I can best describe it's functions. I ran the program and started to tinker with it by creating a false bill note to track. A few keystrokes into the program and the dreaded "SYNTAXERROR IN XXX" popped up. This is not good. I ran the program again and inputted different information, but the same message appeared. Uh oh! I listed the code line given by the Commodore and that very line did a Harry Houdini on me and disappeared. I panicked as a solemn thought hit me: What if I copyrighted a faulty text of program? I went through my files and found a copy of the text of program I originally sent to the Copyright Office and looked on the printed sheet for the missing code line. As sure as cow flatulence the code line was gone; I did copyright a flawed program. For a fleet moment I was madder than a stirred up hornet's nest, then a thought hit me: I was about to try and sell a flawed program to the general Commodore public and I was prevented in doing so by heaven above and the Caretaker thereof.

I sat down with the disk and Commodore and slowly started to work through each syntax one at a time. Some were just missing code lines; others were missing or misdirected GOTOs and GOSUBs. I don't know how long it took but I finally worked all the "bugs" out of the program, but now I was stuck with a new problem: What do I do with a wasted copyright notice on a malfunctioning program? Answer: Nothing. I would have to get another copyright for the repaired work and title it under a different name. I was reluctant to do this since I copyrighted a bogus program in the first place; I didn't want lightning to strike twice, so it sat, never to see the light of day. Only until recently have I brought this program back to the light of day, and even then I was reluctant for the same aforementioned reason. I don't mind showing it at expos and club meetings, but to head to the public with distribution was scary.

What would I do to improve "Obligator Coordinator?" Any improvements that could have been done was put into "The Ledger." I basically left "Obligator Coordinator" alone. I may put "Obligator Coordinator" out as freeware with "The Ledger" as the purchase product. Either way, what I thought was going to be a legal victory for Commodore coders everywhere turned into a nightmare as the whole thing blew up in my face. I know now to investigate a copyright for periodicals so I can make improvements to what I code without having to apply for a different copyright each upgrade.

"Obligator Coordinator" was hard to code since I didn't know how to make half of the features I wanted a reality in what BASIC I understood. I did learn extra commands while coding the work so "Obligator Coordinator" was not a total waste but a learning experience that was treasured for future Commodore programming.

Shift-Clr/Home

Growing Pains Part Siv
(Where I Learned To Code In Style)

Out of all the things we can do with our Commodore brand of computers, nothing seems to be more important to me than word processing and budgeting, and out of those two I put budgeting on top. Usually a good rule of thumb when it comes to budgeting on the Commodore is having a very good to excellent budgeting piece of software, and I found that piece of software in "Run" magazine's type in program, "Money Manager With E-Z Budget" coded by Mr. Day and published around 1989. This Commodore Redneck owes a great deal of his coding knowledge to Mr. Day when it comes to my making the packages I did for helping users to budget on the Commodore via various software aforementioned in previous articles. With the exception of my best friend and Commodore guru, Carl, Mr. Day has taught me the most about programming on the Commodore. The funny part about this whole educational department for me is that Mr. Day and I have never met. In fact, Mr. Day doesn't even know I exist, but his coding of "Money Manager" deserves to be read by every serious Commodore coder who wants to learn a near perfect balance of BASIC, BASIC machine, and algebraic expressions. I've been using Mr. Day's "Money Manager" program for over 25 years and it has kept a great eye on my spending habits and has shown me in more than one instance "leaks" in my spending that needed to be "plugged." But, even great pieces of software have flaws and "Money Manager" was no exception.

It was February 2000, when I sat down at my Commodore 128 and started to work on the first of the month bills. Usually, "Money Manager" asked if this is a new month, and upon pressing "Y" the computer transposes the data from the previous month (like check book balances and ctc.) to the new month. No so this time. The program asked, "Is this the first input to the program?" Odd. That's a beginning of the year function. Upon pressing "N" the

65

program balked and demanded a valid month then sent me back to start up. I entered the same screen again and, to make a long story short, I had to set up for February like I did January inputting data all over again. Upon investigation of the program text, it seemed that "Money Manager" was suffering from a "Y2K" malady and needed to be fixed.

I must admit I was a little nervous to go into the BASIC of the program and start working on the problem. Mr. Day had the maximum amount of functions settled into a minimal amount of code. Any tinkering of that code may set an unbalance and cause the program to crash upon every boot with possibly no hope of recovery. I studied every line of the 71 block long program before zeroing in on the first 25 lines and deciphering that the date stamp lives in these lines. It took me a couple of hours of trial and error and several reboots before I finally got "Money Manager" to cooperate with the new date stamp I installed. What I did in short was change the "mm/yy" stamp into a "mm/yyyy" stamp, then going through the program and change any GOTO or GOSUB references to the old date stamp to agree with my changes. There was a numerical expression of "100" which told the program to stop working in a year stamp past 99 to "10000" so the program would totally agree with years starting from 2000 and beyond.

After making a program like "Money Manager," written by a great master of Commodore code like Rex Day to work beyond it's intended life expectancy, I wanted some cussing credit for my effort. At the beginning of "Money Manager" is the introduction screen which was coded at the beginning of the program (stands to reason). Before I put in the necessary PRINT statements I thought it best to write in Mr. Day as the primary coder and myself for just adding the "Y2K" updates. Also, for anything I wrote or was a contributor to, I included the name of my local Commodore user group, and yet, when all this was done, the intro screen still lacked the necessary information I felt was necessary, so I changed the name of the work from "Money Manager" to "Money Manager 2K," signifying that this work was now compatible with the year 2000 and beyond. Also, as a side bar, I added that "Run" magazine published the original code.

"Money Manager" itself is a great tool with features like an electric checkbook, checkbook analyzer, and department keeper. In the "E-Z Budget" half there is a budget calculator, a future forecaster (you input the numbers and "E-Z Budget" calculates them down), and a break down by department. The setup is simple: At first input you create your own department heads where each input into the electric checkbook *must* go under a heading. As the year progresses you can add departments as you go up to 16 extra inputs, or you can change a department head that is inert into a new active department. The computer saves all your departments to disk and will access all your departments and load them into your Commodore. In "Budget Analysis" all your departments are calculated for the month thus far and printer onto screen or printer. "E-Z Budget" also does an analysis from projected (your guess) to actual (what really went down) to give you an idea on where yours was planned to go and where it actually went. Mr. Day also added handy "Help" messages that refer to the screen currently displayed. Simply go to the screen in question and press "H" and a box in reverse field will appear at the bottom guiding the user as to what to do.

After using "Money Manager With E-Z Budget" for over two decades I've found only two quirks in the work that I personally blame on the publisher of the code text and not on Mr. Day himself: One is that the computer will syntax and crash at one of the "Help" messages, but I don't use the help messages anymore so this is not a cumbersome issue, but for the beginning user of the program it can be a problem. When this happens just type in RUN at the flashing cursor and the program will restart, but any unsaved input will be lost. This brings me to the second problem: If too much data is entered in one sitting without an occasional dump to disk, "Money Manager" will lock up and not even the pressing of RUN/STOP-RESTORE will break the program loop. Here the user must turn off, then turn on the computer and reboot the program. All unsaved data is definitely lost. I've found a way around this is to SAVE after every third or fourth input. It's tedious, it's long, but it is a big headache saver in the end.

As you probably guessed, I would like to call my programs for Commodore the "best written works" available, but with such great Commodore programmers like Mr. Day, Carl, and others past and present, I will have to take a seat in the back of the room.

If you would like a copy of "Money Manager With E-Z Budget" I'm sure an image of it can be found on many Commodore archive websites for free download, but those copies will not have my "Y2K" updates. Then again, we are well past the first decade of the new century so Mr. Day's original code should work fine; but if you want the program with my updates then please send me a self addressed stamped envelope big enough to hold a 5 1/4" disk to the address found on my website (http://elomaster.wix.com/lenardroach) along with $1 USD (to cover the cost of the disk) and I will get a copy to you.

There's no way I can give "Money Manager" due justice in one short article, but if you've been looking for a great, affordable financial piece of Commodore software than Mr. Day's "Money Manager With E-Z Budget" should be what you've been seeking.

Growing Pains Part Octo
(Tying It All Together)

We're coming to the end of my lectures on the Commodore works that I have been blessed with writing and coding. I know this series has helped me as I see there are things in the program texts that I can add or delete to make all these works cooperate with the user in a more friendly way. I look forward to cracking open these works and, with a lot of time and prayer, I hope to have all the changes done before the release of my new book project already under way. If I stay vigilant, especially through the winter months, all these revamped programs should be ready for a Commodore premiere in July 2017.

Even though these programs stand alone quite well on their own, and they sold decently as individual entities, I thought it would be rather groovy to "bundle" some of these programs under one heading and grant access through a menu selector. But even with that I still needed to make a "boot within a boot" to send the user from the menu, to the tie in screen, to the intro screen, to the program itself. The first piggy back, tying in the menu screen to the tie in screen, was easy; I wrote the tie in screen into the boot screen and just used the "Clear Screen" command (the inverted heart) to switch screens between the menu screen and tie in screen. Going from there? That's a completely different story...

When I started working on daisy chaining the menu, intro, and programs together I knew that a standard chaining program that falsified the actual block size of the intro screen wouldn't work; I needed something more flexible when it came to code. In daisy chaining programs, the program overwriting another program must be bigger, other wise the bigger program being overwritten by the smaller program will leave some of the first program behind and try to "merge" the two programs into one, thus creating a hybrid program that no one can use. To further illustrate, let's say that the intro program is 8 blocks long while the boot program is about 25 blocks long. The Commodore will overwrite the first 8 blocks of the new program will overwrite only the first 8 blocks of the 25 block program leaving 17 blocks of code not dealt with like a dangling participle. You run that and you got a mess on your hands. A simple cold restart will fix that if it happens.

I had this problem when working on the intro screen for "TEA 4 2," so I brought my dilemma (back then) to the members of the Commodore Users Group of Kansas City. A semi retired gentlemen we'll call "Ken" for this article approached me after the meeting with a slip of paper in his possession and handed it to me with the following formulas:

PRINTPEEK(46)

POKE46,X:POKE48,X:POKE50,X:POKE52,X

Ken explained. "LOAD the program you want to daisy chain to into memory. On READY type the PRINTPEEK(46) prompt on a blank line. It will give you a number between 1 and 256. Write that number down somewhere, but add 1 to it. Clear the memory of the Commodore by shutting it off then turning it on. Now, LOAD the program you wish to daisy chain from into memory. Make that list of POKE commands the first line of code in your intro program, replacing the X with the number given to you by the PEEK command. Please remember to add 1 to that number. Save the newly altered program and your problem should be solved."

I've used those two formulas ever since and it has never failed. One note I should add to Ken's: If you add or take away even one line of text or code, you'll have to seek a new X factor. If you don't then the old X factor will not recognize the changes and your program that you daisy chained to may crash upon boot. That always sucks ...

Now the problem I have with the menu boot I wrote is that I have the programs reboot back to the main menu by using a simple LOAD command in BASIC. This is a smaller program trying to overwrite a larger program. See above description. The PEEK and POKE codes will not work since each program returning to the menu is of different sizes. I'm presently experimenting with two options: I'm trying to use the program with the most block's PEEK number and add it to the beginning of the menu program and see if that will work or seeing if a simple CLR command at the end of each major program will give it a completed loop. Without a fix, the programs will only overwrite themselves a few times then the Commodore will crash and a cold restart will be needed. Apparently each overwrite, no matter how successful, leaves a bit or two of data behind until it grows significant and causes the crash. Needless to say the whole thing works to a point so I'm satisfied, but not completely.

With all of this work of tying all five programs up into one conglomeration a title for the package escapes me. I just called it what it was: "The 5 Program Bonus Disk." I like it. Precise. Concise. It'll do. However, before it goes up for sale to the public I have to make some changes to the programs (see previous articles) and write documentation for all the programs in the package.

I found writing this series fun and thought provoking. Some of the ideas I've mentioned throughout spawned from writing this series. My point behind these lectures is to hopefully instigate *you*, dear reader, to start working afresh on your Commodore, and if you already are, to invite you to keep on keeping on.

Shift-Clr/Home

TITLE: Programming In BASIC -- A Root Canal With No Anesthetic

POINT OF ORIGIN: Commodore Free Magazine

MODE: Story essay

SYNOPSIS: Lenard describes in good detail the frustration in trying to find the most minuscule of bugs in a program that can run you over like an out of control freight train. Lenard also tries to capture the elation of succeeding in solving the BASIC, only to realize he burned his night away . Direct as well as lighthearted.

Shift-Clr/Home

Programming In BASIC – A Root Canal With No Anesthetic

"How in poodoo did this happen?"

It was about 1:30 in the morning on a cold Tuesday in February. I sat in my leather like office chair with the broken wheel, staring at the screen of my Commodore computer wondering what this mess of text was on the monitor. This is not what I wrote in the command lines to tell the Commodore 128 to do. The question then became: What **did** I tell the Commodore to do?

I know that part of the problem was fatigue. I had been up since six in the morning to get ready for work, then worked a fifteen hour shift on the job before I got to come home and relax, but I knew that this project on the Commodore has been waiting on me since before Christmas and needed to be started, so after resting and unwinding with some cold sandwiches from the refrigerator and a video short or two on YouTube, I left the living room to sit at the Commodore in the Roach Center's dedicated computer room.

I sat at the Commodore desk, which is located on the south wall of the room; my son's Mac Mini and Xbox One were on the north wall. He was already in the room using the Center's wireless Internet to connect and play with some online friends, so as to not to disturb his game play, I grabbed my iPhone 4 and headphones that were nearby and started playing some of my Electric Light Orchestra over the headphones while I started the task of programming what I needed into the Commodore.

The problem in question was a subroutine that I was adding to an already existing program that I have tried to sell at the Las Vegas Commodore computer convention a couple of years ago. I only made a couple of sales on the program, but decided that for this year's convention I would make the program more user friendly by adding more subroutines that granted more access to different needs that, I thought, the user would need. One of those subroutines was a directory reader written by the late Mr. Butterfield that he gave out on a disk. It came in a collection of disks that, I believe, came directly from Commodore itself back in the day. I know that the program was copyrighted so I gave credit to Mr. Butterfield in the REM statements included in the program text. Mr. Butterfield's directory reading program needed some slight modifications to allow it to work with the needs of my program's main function, but before I did that I searched all the local Commodore clubs, boards, and websites looking for a better directory reading program that worked as a subroutine to a bigger conglomeration of the work. Out of the dozen or so directory readers I found around, only Mr. Butterfield's directory reader would cooperate best with what I was trying to accomplish in BASIC.

What I saw on my screen that night made no sense. Instead of printing the directory's contents on the screen in a book fashion (left to right), it printed the information in a column (up to down), with each letter of the title of each file in a straight line. I knew I missed something in the translation of the subroutine from the master disk to the program I wanted to put it in. I know that some advanced Commodore programmers know how to embed a subroutine into a program without having to enter it in a line at a time; I did not, so I know that the problem existed in what I put where in the subroutine.

The first thing I did was print off a copy of the working subroutine using my Star NX-1000C printer. I did this by loading the subroutine into the Commodore then, on a blank line on the screen I typed the following string:

OPEN3,4:CMD3:LIST:PRINT#3:CLOSE3

This gave to me a copy of the program in printed form. At first glance of the subroutine and what I had of the same subroutine on my screen, everything was correct. Just to make sure that my Commodore was freaking out I rebooted the machine and loaded a copy of "TEA v4.2" which uses the same directory reader by Mr. Butterfield. I accessed the directory in "TEA v4.2" just fine and the display on the monitor was perfect. That proved it; the Commodore machine was fine and there was no corruption of the directory reader, therefore, the corruption must be in my translation of the subroutine into the new program.

Mr. Butterfield was an expert programmer. He knew that there should be no waste of space when it came to coding on the Commodore. Even though his directory reading subroutine is several lines in length, every letter, punctuation, and algebraic expression had to mean something. I started the erasing and copying the subroutine several times just to be sure I wasn't doing something wrong and each time I got the same up and down display of text on the screen. I knew I was missing something, but I didn't know what. It had to be something small; so insignificant that I am walking it over each and every time I copied the subroutine into the Commodore line by line. I even printed out the entire program where the directory reader was going just to see if there was any way the program itself was looping into the subroutine and causing an error. Something else I found frustrating; the computer didn't give me an ERROR IN LINE...so I could go right to the offending line of code and fix the problem. According to the Commodore, the program was right and the machine was able to read it without a hiccup.

2 am...3am...4 am; the time kept quickly getting away from me. In two hours I had to get up and start work, but this frustrating little difficulty in the program was really getting on my nerves to a point that I was taking this programming error personally. I knew I would be as worthless as a zombie on a quiz show if I didn't knock this fervent searching for the error and go to bed, but I also knew

that even if I did go to bed I would lie there thinking about what it was that I possibly did wrong and not sleep a wink. However, by 4:30 am I was resolved that this error would never be found and I would go to bed. However, before checking in for 90 minutes of sleep, I would look at all the printed programs one more time and see if I could find the error. I think I even shot a prayer up to heaven asking The Almighty to show this poor, exhausted fool where his mistake was in copying the subroutine.

At 4:12 and 42 seconds on the next day in February, I saw the error. It was so small that my tired and reddening eyes was looking over it time and time again. I felt like the worst of the worst of whatever derogatory name I could call myself, and I called myself that several times before I went back to the keyboard and started typing. The error? I forgot to add a semi-colon at the end of one of the lines of text in the subroutine. Without the semi-colon telling the Commodore to carry on to the next line what was written in the offending line, the program insisted that this line of data was concluded and went onto the next line in the code, thus creating the up and down printing style when the program listed the directory on the screen. I added the missing semi-colon to the line in question, saved the program to disk using the "save with replace" option I read about in my copy of the Programmer's Reference Guide, then ran the program. I selected the number on the screen that told the Commodore to read the directory onto the screen. There to my relief the display on the monitor showed what was on the disk from left to right. Victory has been seized and the entire program was saved, including the directory reading subroutine.

I was done with coding for the rest of the day, and probably for the next several days. With the adrenaline gone out of my system with the discovery of the mistake, my fatigue took full control of me, I shut off the Commodore and staggered into bed, flopping face down onto the pillow. I knew that for the next hour and fifteen minutes, I would sleep the sleep of a victorious knight who won the prize from the maiden's hand after a day's worth of jousting, and sleep I did, not knowing when I would wake up; hopefully at the appropriate time, but I forgot to set the alarm during my short celebration over finding and fixing the code error...

The phone rang next to my bed for only God knows how long, but its tone was loud enough to arouse me out of my slumber. I rolled over to face my night stand where my phone rested each night before I went to bed. Still tired, I almost rolled over onto Dover, my yellow striped tabby cat who snuggled up to me in the middle of the morning. With weak fingers, I fumbled with the phone, trying to find the answer button on it. After a couple of seconds, I finally answered the ringing.

"Hullo?" I said into the receiver in a groggy voice.

"Lenard, are you coming to work today?" It was dispatch.

Aw nuts! I looked at my wall clock in the room. It read 9:30.

"Yeah, yeah, Steve, I'm ready to go." I lied out my exhausted face; I was still in bed and in my sleeping clothes, and Dover was lying next to me. "What do you have for me?"

"I've got a ten o'clock downtown that needs to go to Lee's Summit by 11:30 and then pick up at Venture Industries while in Lee's Summit a couple of packages that needs to be in Olathe by 1:30, but be sure to pick up the bank bags at 10th and McGee before you head to Olathe. Do you got all that?"

"Yeah, yeah, I got it." I lied again. I didn't even have the strength to pull the covers off of me or move Dover out of the way so I could get up.

Steve continued on. "I'll send the orders to you over your cell phone. You've got a half hour to get downtown; better hop to it."

"Yeah, okay. I'm on my way." I lied a third time. I was just moving Dover out of my way, kicking my covers off me and scrambling out of the bed. I quickly hung up the phone. The adrenaline that was motivating me the night before once again kicked in as I rushed around to get my uniform and pants on. In the short space of five minutes I was dressed and heading for the front door. As I passed by the Roach Center's computer room, I stopped and gave my Commodore computer stand a long stare, remembering what we had been through the night before, and I smiled, remembering the victory I won over the problem yesterday. I tapped on the door frame with my hand. "Later today, my friend," I said to the silent machine sitting on the opposite end of the room. "We'll do this again later today." I grabbed my winter coat off its hook in the living room and headed out the door to begin my day smiling, knowing that I will indeed have a meeting with my Commodore – later today.

TITLE: Thanks For The Memory

POINT OF ORIGIN: Commodore Free Magazine

MODE: Article

SYNOPSIS: Lenard gives a written "thank you" to all who have endured and do endure, a form of persecution by those who think that Commodores are best to be used as doorstops, boat anchors, or polluting our landfills. He also praises those with broader minds to take Commodore further than what was probably intended.

Shift-Clr/Home

Thanks For The Memory

When it comes down to the BASICs of life (forgive the pun), you can never get away far from the trusty Commodore computer. Usually, when it comes to learning a truth or two about anything, I have to go over the data about a thousand times before things start to settle into my stubborn frame of mind. I think that might be the problem of some of us in the over fifty generation; we get stuck in our ways and we'll swing from a rope around our necks before we try something new. Heh, you should have seen me switching from cassettes to CDs; I honestly thought that the Japanese were trying to take over America through our media because they were still honked off about Hiroshima and Nagasaki. The music industry could kiss my fat, flabby, flatulent fanny before I pull away from my trusty cassettes. Now I have no cassettes and a collection of CDs that are heading for obsolete as digital media begins to wind it's way through both the music and movie industry. No doubt about it, this Redneck has to start stepping up to the times.

But somehow, this rule of "upgrade from obsolete" doesn't apply too well when it comes to the fantastic and flexible Commodore line of computers. The 21st century is an amazing time to be a Commodore computer user. With the advancement being made on all the upgrades, both in hardware and software, to computers it seems like companies like Microsoft and Apple create stuff just to pitch the same stuff no more than six months to a year after creation -- but not with Commodore. While PC hardware hits the trash due to "incompatibility" with itself, Commodore latches onto what it already has and welcomes to its genre all the hardware and software upgrades that can be made without so much as a chip finding its way into the local landfill.

I take my hat off to all those who manage to take the Commodore line of products and integrate with the machines so many new ideas -- too many of those ideas to be mentioned in this short of a piece. The men and women of Commodore don't know how much this Redneck admires and appreciates their efforts to keep this 8 bit machine running in leagues with Microsoft, Apple, Linux, and the like. It makes me wonder what in heaven's name they go through to make such devices like the 64DTV, SuperCPU, along with the software to make it work. I know in my personal experience all I do is dream up and idea (usually out of necessity), then start coding on my trusty Commodore 128. I've seen some coders use special diagrams called "templates" or "paradigms" to help them think through some of their ideas to make sure that, before any data goes down into the machine, they know where each routine goes into the entire package. I've tried templates in the past and all they do is get me confused with all the "IF A$ = NO THEN go here" and so on. I just sit down and start writing code, visualizing the entire program in my head but not as a complete program. I see everything in subroutines and write down each subroutine into Commodore BASIC before I go on to the next area. Do any of you remember the old 1979 movie "Star Trek The Motion Picture" where this vast machine called "Vger" is built around a small Earth probe that was launched back in the 20th century? My programming is like building the "Vger" probe. I start with the small subroutine that is the nucleus or heart of the entire program then build around that to a full blown functioning, menu driven, multi-selective, useful piece of Commodore software. Are there hardships along the way? You bet!

I think I've mentioned this before somewhere, but I was told a long time ago before I started to get serious with anything that I put down on paper, be it an article like this or typing BASIC code on the Commodore, that, if you don't have a skin thick enough to handle the oncoming criticisms (and they *will* come, that's a guarantee) for anything that you write, then don't write anything at all. Keep it to yourself in a personal journal or diary. Words come back to haunt you, especially when those words are emblazoned on the printed page, and, thanks to the Internet, shown on the media as well. Nobody can just be "flippant" anymore without having some group, organization, or individual getting hacked off and the next thing you are doing is scrambling for cover and the verbal shrapnel flies. I was given advice about what to do with *those* types of people, too -- let them rant, rave, curse, and swear all they want. Don't so much as give them the time of day, if you can avoid doing so. Chances are mostly good that you, as the writer or coder, have stumbled across something that the raver wishes they could have done or said, and since they were too slow on the draw to come up with what was done first, they choose to slam you instead, trying to steal from you any limelight you may have generated. When you answer such a person you are literally giving them that light they so richly desire. So far I've been able to lob my verbal hand grenades far enough from the critical crowd that I rarely get much back flak, but I do get some. Once in a while a reader of my Commodore spiel or a user of one of my programs will catch my rantings and give a scathing review of what I've done. I only respond to said person if I am asked to by the editor of the magazine or software company to which the note was sent, other than that, I leave them alone to rant, avoiding them as much as I can to avoid adding more fuel to the fire. Don't get me wrong, it took me a *long* time to develop this hardness of hide. As a novice writer back in 1995 I got a lot of felgercarb from the editor of the Kansas City Commodore newsletter to which, in response, I would hide in a darkened corner and suck my thumb with tears running down my face, and I wouldn't write a thing for a year or two. After I "toughen" up a bit (ha!) I would write a blurb or two and see who would slap my hand for saying such a thing. If my hand was slapped I was back into the fetal position; if nobody said anything then I would write more, sticking my word processing "toe" out there waiting for it to get ran over. A baby? Yes, I was, but I learned.

Now here I am, twenty years, countless articles, a few programs, and three books later and I am admiring all those who went through this crud before me. I've heard some horror stories over my time of people in Commodore who have recieved terrible treatment from Commodore at large. To them I say, "Thanks" for having the voracity and tenacity to stand and keep standing against all those critics over all these years, and yet refusing to be swayed by those who believe that tearing you down is the best way to build themselves up. I've been told by others that, "I don't stir the sewage enough to cause a stink" and that's why I'm left mostly alone. This could be. The Rabbi Paul once said, "As much as it is within you, be at peace with all men." I seek to do that as much as possible, but I know that the time is coming when I will step on the right Commodore toes and things will start flying like it was the Gulf War all over again. It's like my working at all these convenience stores since 1990, I have yet to be held up on my shift, and for this record I am thankful, but my day is coming. I am also thankful for the few toes I've stepped on in the Commodore universe, and for those I have, I've been able to ignore.

With all this sentimental hooplah said and in print, I need to urge future scribes and coders who so dare as to sit down in front of Dad's or Grandpa's Commodore wondering how in blazes you boot this thing, or if you are that Dad or Grandpa with something to say about this "not so archaic" machine or even an idea for a great piece of software or invent a fantastic piece of hardware, to no longer be shy or backwards and get started on your project. I used to think that I could write a book a year to keep up with "the big dogs," but I found out that those "big dogs" have a stenography staff several desks long and a publisher already in line waiting to use the author's name on a product that would surely bring in a profit from just for the name alone. Some writers even get an advance royalty. Me? I just sit quietly in my computer room typing and editing everything I do on one lone sentinel of a Commodore 128 waiting patiently for the next idea to come to mind so I can proceed forward with my silent career. This may not be you, but you will never know until you sit your fanny down and join the ranks of the Commodore herd, and be heard.

For those who have blazed my Commodore trail ahead of me I say, "Thanks for the memory," no matter what size...

Shift-Clr/Home

TITLE: Why I Use A Commodore

POINT OF ORIGIN: Commodore Free Magazine

MODE: Essay

SYNOPSIS: Lenard gives reasons why he still uses a Commodore even though there are more powerful machines on the market. He also gives a short summary on what happened to some Commodore computers and disk drives he was given. Light hearted and entertaining.

Shift-Clr/Home

Why I Use A Commodore

Sometimes a person has to think as to why they do the things that they do. For some people, they do things out of habit; others do things because that was how they were taught; still others do because they seemingly have no choice. This is not so when it comes to the Commodore brand of computer. Those who still use the machine use it for various reasons. This piece is about why I personally use a Commodore even now in the 21st century when there are faster and higher memory machines on the market.

AFORDABILITY – When it comes to the Commodore in the 21st century, the machines affordability instantly comes into play. Many a person are willing to dispose of their perfectly good working Commodores for a mere pittance, and in many cases, the units, drives, and other peripherals come absolutely free. Many former Commodore owners only want the units out of the house to make room for more modern computers or, in more humorous cases, the fiance or wife wants the unit out because it is an "eyesore." Whatever the case may be, Commodore computers are affordable and in big supply in many areas of the world; a person only has to know where to locate these units and then collect them for whatever use can be planned.

SAFETY – The Commodore seems to be the safest computer on the market. With computers, mainframes full of personal information, or any other modern computer problems, the Commodore seems to be devoid of such infections. When I was writing "Run/Stop-Restore," I wanted to add a chapter on viruses that exist for the Commodore 64 or 128. When I put the request out on FIDOnet for such information, nobody answered me. Even if someone were to be able to sabotage the Commodore by way of software, a quick shut down of the machine and reboot will clear any infections. I did encounter a piece of software back in the 90's that was given to me from a collection that had a Trojan horse

91

protector, which, when I booted the disk on my personal 128, a message appeared stating that this disk was not allowed to be booted on my machine, suspected that I pirated the software, and went into disk reformatting procedures. However, hacking computing machines was active way back in the 80's, for I had from the same collection a disk containing a list of credit card numbers for anyone to use. Naturally, these numbers were stolen and people were suppose to use the stolen card numbers to buy more Commodore products. I took that copy of the disk to the local police department, who investigated the numbers and luckily all the numbers on the disk were already turned in to the associating credit card companies and subsequently had the accounts that belong to and shut down.

Also, I consider the Commodore (especially the stock models) Internet safe, meaning that I don't have to worry about children getting onto the Commodore and looking at sites that they shouldn't be on. A person has to physically load a pornographic disk into the Commodore disk drive and boot it in order to look at the scenes, and these disks can be put away under lock and key and the key put in a safe place before a child can get to them. When it came to my own children playing on the Commodore, I had no worries even though the computer had a modem for BBS browsing; there were no place the kids could go to look at any suggestive material. I could leave them alone to play any games or use any educational material I had in my collection. With today's computers it's a simple game of point and click for a person or even a child to look at pornographic or other suggestive material.

COMPATIBILITY – You read that word right, dear reader, compatibility; and this coming from the comedian who has written in the past that Commodores and PCs will never be of any use together. This was before I was introduced to the IBM/Commodore translator program, "Big Blue Reader," and any other styles of software that do the same thing. This program will, literally, transpose information (in my case, manuscripts, texts, and other writings) out of Commodore word processors and into a readable text format easily understood by today's modern PCs and, if necessary, back again. During my early years as editor of the Fresno Commodore User Group's newsletter, "The Interface," I used "Big Blue Reader" to take all the PC word processed text and convert them to Commodore GeoWrite for cutting and pasting into a Commodore created newsletter. Now in these recent years, I make "The Interface" on a PC by taking my Commodore GeoWrite text and converting it to PC, but believe me, it is easier to use and understand the Commodore set up than the PC for making newsletters as I am still learning how to make the papers into an eye catching, informative publication using the more modern machine.

PANACHE – Do you want to impress the younger generation, especially those who are in their pre-teens and younger? Tell them about how you use a computer that existed well before they were born. This is fun to do when you can show them an actual copy of the computer and how it works. In my opinion, most children are drawn to the complexity of how to use the older machines when all they have to do today is either click on an icon or tap on an app. Most kids are not aware of megabytes and gigabytes but only that there is enough room on the hard drive to store the new upload. This fun I got to experience when I got three working Commodore 128s along with the necessary cables and peripherals. I thought I could make a gag gift out of one of the C128s and a couple of drives and give them to a co-worker who family happens to be up to date on all the latest electronic gadgets. When she got the C128 I told her that if she didn't want it she could sell it on eBay for about $100 if she marketed it right. I was surprised when I found out she actually loved the C128 and her family couldn't wait to hook it up and start having fun with all this old technology. Her husband, a true man, tried his best to hook up the Commodore without instructions but has failed time and time again to get everything hooked up and the machine to boot. It looks like I'll have to make my very first Commodore house call and show them how to assemble the Commodore and all its drives and serial bus cables. It's been a long time since I taught Commodore BASIC to anyone, but it should prove to be interesting.

The second Commodore went to the church that I attend as a prize the kids in children's church could "buy" with Sunday School Bucks. The Sunday School superintendent was totally interested in getting the C128 from me and promised to put a low price on the machine so the kids could afford it. I don't know if the kids are interested in such technology but it will be interesting to see the reaction of all those children as they gaze upon such a device and ask the teacher, "What is that?" The kids know that I write most of the skits we adults do for them on the Commodore computer so now they have a chance to have a copy of that unit for their very own.

The third and final Commodore 128 will be going to the son of a very dear friend of mine who has already passed from this world. This friend was the one who started me into Commodore was back in 1990 and has taught me a lot of things about the machine before he died. I found his son through Facebook and we started talking. He has a lot of questions about his father, but one thing he remembered about his dad was the fact that he operated a Commodore 128. When I told him over the Internet that I had a copy of that machine in my house sitting around doing nothing, he was interested in seeing what a real one looked like. I told him he could have this unit as a gift from me. He wasn't ecstatic about getting the unit as the co-worker was, but it's more of a nostalgia thing for him as he will be handling something that his father once had. He has no memory of his father since his dad passed when he was three, so anything this kid could get about his dad is something of a connection with a man long gone but not forgotten.

VERSATILITY – Never have I used something that with just a simple swap of the disk you can change the machine from a word processor into a gaming device. Sure, today's computers can do the same thing and all from one or more windows, but when it comes to the best computer ever made, it seems like more of a miracle that this one machine, with its 64K or 128K of memory and space, can do so much, and here in the 21st century it is so affordable that it's not even funny. Games and productivity software is selling on many websites for a large fraction less than what the products were when they were new. Also, what really blows the balding skull of this out of work comedian is that right now while you are reading this, someone somewhere on our planet is developing more games and productivity software for the Commodore. Reports are all over the Internet and in various newsletters and magazines that still support the machine of these new developments. This is a great time to discover or rediscover the Commodore computer all over again.

I'm sure there are many more reasons that lots of people can think of as to how groovy it is to be a Commodore user in the 21st century. I've only listed a few in the above paragraphs, but a lot more has not been said, but for whatever the reason, Commodore still is the best computer on the market bar none. I'm thankful to be a part of the Commodore universe.

Shift-Clr/Home

TITLE: A Commodore Christmas

POINT OF ORIGIN: Commodore Free Magazine

MODE: Story

SYNOPSIS: Lenard tells a humorous tale of how he received his first 5 1/4" disk drive.

Shift-Clr/Home

A Commodore Christmas

Going over the last fifteen years of using the Commodore and
Commodore products, nothing gave me more surprise than that one
Christmas day back in the early 90s when my then wife threw me
for a Commodore loop.

When I got my first Commodore 64, it was a hand-me-down from
a family friend who no longer had a use for the machine. Whether
she updated her computer to something more modern or not I
cannot say, all I know is that I asked for a computer so I could
word process my skits and plays and she saw herself in a position
to surrender one to me. This poor C64 was the bare bones basic
machine as one could get. It had an old MPS 802 non-graphic
printer and used a tape drive as the software transfer device. This
was not a problem at first since I never used a Commodore before
and cassettes were $3.99 for a pack of three at the local K-Mart.
Everything was very affordable for me to run this set up.
Unfortunately, I took over the living room television as my
monitor so anytime the wife wanted to watch a show, I would have
to log off the Commodore by spending the fifteen minutes or so
saving my work to tape. Again, the makers of the computer forsaw
this and made the RF modulator to change between TV and
computer so Mrs. Roach could watch half of her program before I
had to switch back to computer to check if it was done saving. Of
course to verify that my data was saved to tape, I had to rewind the
tape to the front and tell the computer to verify data, and the fifteen
minute process would start over. Again it was back to TV to catch
the second half of the program being viewed. I think you get the
idea how this love triangle worked as, every once in a while, I
would have to bow out of computing to give Mrs. Roach her time
to watch TV.

As the 5 1/4" disks were becoming more and more popular, the use
of tape drive programs became harder and harder to find at the

local computer store. Type-in programs from magazines that didn't require the use of a disk drive were the best way for the Roach family to get games and productivity programs for the Commodore 64 back in the early days, but even then, with Speedscript 3.0 as my main word processor and a stack of a dozen cassette tapes with games and manuscripts, the need for a disk drive was becoming more and more prevalent. Christmas was coming up that year, so I put a bug into everyone's ear that the one thing that Lenard wanted for Christmas was a 1541 (or its 5.25" equivalent) disk drive. Day after day I didn't stop talking about getting a Commodore disk drive for the holiday. Some people I talked to actually told me to "shut the **** up" about this disk drive.

Ladies and gentlemen, I was anal expressive when it came to letting people know about my need for a disk drive so I could continue my work as a (hopefully) aspiring writer. I told both friends and family alike as well, as I am sure, some total strangers. Finally, in a bit of frustration, my wife looked at me in disgust and told me that I am getting a typewriter for Christmas and that was that. I didn't need a typewriter! I had a word processor in the Commodore and I could do what I needed with that, so again I persued the need for a disk drive not a typewriter. When a present ended up under the tree that was about as big as a manual typewriter, I surrendered. Instead of getting the all-important disk drive I needed, I got a typewriter, and I'd better get that thought into my head. Once in a while, over the next few weeks I mentioned the disk drive, and each and every time Mrs. Roach shut me down with the typewriter under the tree. I was such a richard cranium over getting this device that the wife had to remind me that this holiday was mainly for the kids so I should start think about our 4-year-old son and what we should get him for the holiday. I consented and, acting like a 4-year-old for the rest of the Advent season, I went around to the various department stores with the wife looking at toys, clothes, and games for my son. Before the actual holiday arrived, I got my head out of my anus long enough to see a little daylight and get Mrs. Roach some things for Christmas. But oh, the fact that I was not getting that strongly coveted disk drive for Christmas burned in my soul was searing at me. I played back track for about two weeks telling everybody who knew I wanted a disk drive that I was getting a typewriter for Christmas. Most said that such a device was cheaper to get than the disk drive, and they were right; even parts for a manual typewriter was cheaper at the office supply store than going to the Commodore store in Overland Park, Kansas and getting a $210 disk drive. Others told me that I deserved what I got for being such an ass head about the disk drive so the downgrade was good for my pride and ego.

Christmas Day finally arrived. As my wife's parents, my mom, my son, my wife and I sat around the tree, I grabbed the typewriter box first, asking if I should open it up since I knew what it was. Mrs. Roach chided me, saying that it will be the LAST present you open since I was being such a baby about it for so many weeks. One by one and person by person, presents were passed out, opened, admired, and in some cases tried on for admiration. My in-laws were nice enough to get me a ten-pack of cassettes for both my music as well as my Commodore tape drive. I thanked them sincerely for the gift, knowing that the tape drive was going to be my computer companion for quite a while. With all the presents finally opened but the typewriter, I asked if I can open it now. Mrs. Roach had the packages marked 1 through 5, with 5 being the typewriter itself. She told me to open the packages starting with number one and working my way down to the typewriter. One by one, each package was opened. One package was a disk notcher, which I didn't know what I was going to do with it. One was a disk file box, which I thought was to be used to organize my tapes since they were strewn all over the TV stand as I used them. Two packages were a stack of multi-colored 5.25" disks, which had me curious -- could package #5 be ...? No, I was told specifically and adamantly that I was not getting the disk drive. Chances were likely that Mrs. Roach got me a word processor that required the use of 5.25 disks to save the information on.

Now it was time to access package #5, the big one. I picked up the box and started to take off the wrapping. The ever-famous "chicken lips" C= glanced back at me, like saying, "Hello." As more of the paper came off, it was clear that I had been royally and perfectly duped. After the paper came off, my eyes started to fill with tears as in my hands was a brand-new, in the box, Commodore 1541 disk drive. I asked the wife, "How come so small?" She explained to me that this disk drive was a recent upgrade to the larger 1541 drives that required less space to run. Behind the 1541 logo was the double I symbol, indicating that this was the up-to-date 1541-II disk drive.

I went into meltdown mode instantly, hugging and kissing my wife over and over again as I showed her the disk drive she got me. I flashed the box to my in-laws, who didn't know what to think of the weird machine. My poor father-in-law, for a moment, thought I was disappointed that I got the disk drive and was ready to go out on December 26th and get me the typewriter. My mother-in-law explained that this was exactly what I was wanting for Christmas and not to bother a thing. My wife; so clever was she that she even convinced my son that the disk drive was indeed a typewriter so anytime I quizzed him about the "big" package, he would tell me it was a typewriter. This woman truly loved me, even through my own stupidity. I spent the rest of Christmas day working on transferring all my programs and writings, one at a time, from tape to disk and making my now useless tapes ready for use in my car as music tapes.

But this party isn't over yet. A day of retribution was at hand...

As life slowly started back up the following day, I ran into co-workers who smiled and asked, "So, how do you like the new typewriter?" I looked at them with a smile and said that she got me a very special disk drive for my computer. "Yeah, we know," they said. "She had that thing bought since early November." Douche bags! Everybody knew I had that disk drive coming and they let me play the fool!

As the weeks wore on, I got phone calls from family and friends every day asking the same question. I can't believe that I made a butt face out of myself when Mrs. Roach had everything under control the whole time. I have never eaten so much shoe leather over something in my life, but I deserved it. From there on out I was thankful to get anything for the holidays and never questioned what was in packages again.

That 1541-II disk drive is well past gone now. I wore out the heads from all the constant use of loading and saving programs. I remember taking that drive to our Kansas City Commodore fix it guy several times and he replaced everything but the casing. That poor drive never worked right like it came from the factory that one Christmas day, but this much I'll say -- Commodore knew how to build computers during the day. No wonder I say, "Long live Commodore!"

Shift-Clr/Home

TITLE: If Jesus Owned A Commodore

POINT OF ORIGIN: Reset Magazine

MODE: Story

SYNOPSIS: Lenard tells a fictional story based on real events where he helped a co-worker boost sales in her department by using just his Commodore and a video tape recorder. Funny and touching.

Shift-Clr/Home

If Jesus Owned A Commodore

Even though I got into the Commodore hobby habit *very* late in the game (1988, I think) doesn't mean I didn't have fun with the people around me who either didn't own a computer, owned a machine manufactured by the competition of the time, or didn't know the computer they owned could do such amazing things. I was working at a department store in 1989 as a custodian (we'll call the store "Pickles" for the rest of this article to protect any innocents) and I think what surprised everyone there was why this guy was pushing a broom on the floor and not a pen in an IT office? Even though I was still a novice when it came to computers I was the HMIC of same at Pickles. Only the true IT guys at Pickles knew I wasn't all that and a bag of chips, but they also were a bunch of wise guys who usually asked me to look at a register that was malfunctioning or a VCR that didn't play, and if I couldn't fix it then they came out as white knights and saved the day. I didn't care; I didn't have to scrub somebody's defecation off a bathroom wall when I was called onto the floor. Reprieve!

One of my regular routines at Pickles was to wet mop the wooden walkway that encompassed the Juniors Department like a jogging track. In the blouse and skirt area there were three televisions mounted side by side about seven and a half feet above the floor and embedded flush into the wall. I believe the TVs were the 26" models. The department manager kept playing the same old music videos in the VCR to where people were just sick of it, employees as well as frequenting customers. Sales were sagging. I thought to myself, "What can I, as a broom pusher and a mop slinger, do to perk this up?" Was it my duty or responsibility to do anything about their video display? No, but for some insane reason this thing was bothering me and I wanted to do something about it. Also, I was sick of the same video, too. I had to see it every time I swept it and wet mopped it.

I went home and started to peruse my collection of videos. They couldn't show movies or TV shows on those monitors or else be in breach of copyright laws, and that's all I had. I crossed over to my desk where sat my recently acquired Commodore 64 computer. I stared at the unit, using it as a focal point for my eyes while my mind pondered elsewhere. For a fleet moment after hypnotically gazing at the machine for several minutes, the computer came to mind. I've seen computer stores in the mall use a video they made themselves of games they wanted to sell and show it on TVs in the display glass. Why don't I do the same?

I went into the living room and disconnected the VCR from the TV and hooked it up to my Commodore 64 and monitor in my office. A quick test and I saw everything was working properly. My first major video production was going to be none other than me playing "Cosmic Relief," a video game my wife got me for Christmas the year before and I had beaten several times. I was going to impress people with my skills of being a gamer!

Before the game began, I had to show off the impressive Commodore home screen and type in, real slow, the LOAD command that would boot "Cosmic Relief". After a minute of displaying the intro screen I went into game play. A summary of the game: A meteor is coming to destroy the Earth and The Professor sends you out to collect all the parts necessary to build a deflector shield within a certain time frame. If the counter reaches zero and the deflector shield isn't built, then Earth is destroyed; collect all that The Professor needs within the allotted time and Earth is saved by a giant flipper that is found in every pinball machine.

As usual, The Almighty Omnipotent Creator Of Everything Groovy And Cool had other plans for my "Let's Play" video debut. Instead of beating the game like I planned, time ran out and Earth was destroyed. "Ah nuts!" I screamed. "The video is ruined!"

The game went to the start screen again. I was about to stop the recording when a still, small voice whispered to me, "Don't. Play again." I knew I had plenty of tape left so I started again. This time I saved the Earth with plenty of time to spare. I rewound the video tape and watched it through after I put the VCR back into the living room. The failure to win gave the video a human quality. It was better than planned. I packed the tape in my lunch box and waited for work tomorrow...

It was 8:00 am the next morning. I just finished sweeping the circular walkway by the Junior Miss department and went back to the janitorial storage to get my mop and bucket, and the video. I walked up to the department manager, a beautiful Americanized Asian woman that was built in all the right places (we'll call her Miss Hung for now) and gave her the video.

"What's this?" she asked me with no slur in her accent.

"It's a video I made for the department last night," I answered.

"Is it a music video?"

"No. It's a video of the monitor and my Commodore 64 as I played a game."

She shook her head and gave the video back to me.

"I appreciate the effort, Lenard, but the Operations Manager won't allow me to play nothing but music videos on the TV," she said in a woeful tone. "Thanks anyway."

She turned away from me and resumed preparing her department to open and I dragged my feet back to storage to put the video back. I placed it carefully in then slammed the lid shut on my Igloo Lunch Cooler. I grit my teeth. A wise captain of a certain starship we all should know would say one day, "I didn't come all this way just to be stopped by something like this!" A plan was formulating in my crazy cranium; it was so crazy that it just might work, but I had to wait until tomorrow to execute it. If it works then everybody will be happy; if not, then a few fannies, my own included, will be fried....

It was now 6:00 am the following morning. I entered Pickles Department Store through the employee entrance with my Igloo Lunch Cooler tightly tucked under my left arm. After timing in, I bolted through the store and downstairs to the Junior Miss Department. With minimal lighting, I fumbled through drawers looking for the remotes to the TVs and the VCR. After finding them, I turned on all the electronics, ejected the already super worn out tape and put in mine. In a few short seconds "Cosmic Relief" was playing in the department. I put all the remotes back and, with stealth, grabbed my lunch box and walked away....

"Hey, Lenard," the Dock Manager said, "check this out."

It was 8:00 am and I was just starting my dust mop run of the Juniors Department. Half of the dock personnel were standing in the Junior Miss area and looking up. For a minute I thought the area was on fire, but there would be more widespread panic and less standing around. I leaned my dust handle on a jeans rack and walked over to them. The video of "Cosmic Relief" I inserted into the VCR was playing through for the who know what time.

"This is cool," one person said.

"I've never seen a video game made into a video before," said another.

"How'd they do this?" a third asked.

"How did who do what?" came a stern voice from down the aisle. Coming towards us was the Operations Manager (we'll call him "Dick Sargent" for this article) with Miss Hung close behind. They both crowded themselves through all of us and stood in front and watched the video for a few seconds. Miss Hung spun her head around making her ebony strands of hair flow evenly through the air, to give me the ever famous Female Glare Of Instant Disintegration. They watched the video for a few seconds more, then Dick addressed Miss Hung, "Where did you get this? You know only music videos are allowed to be played on these screens."

I was about to speak up, but before I could utter a word someone in the crowd chimed in: "Just a second, Mr. Sargent," he said, "this is a music video of sorts."

"It's got music, though it is done on a computer of some kind," said one person.

"And it is a video, it's just the video of a game being played," echoed another. The crowd mumbled in agreement. Dick crossed his arms, stroked his handlebar style mustache, and watched the video for a few more minutes. He again turned to Miss Hung.

"All right, Miss Hung, I'll let this ride for now, but if I get one complaint from a customer then I'll have it pulled." Dick turned to address the crowd that grew while our backs were turned and clapped his hands. "Back to work, people! The store opens at nine!"

The crowd quickly dispersed. I stood around because I knew I had to face my Day of Retribution with Miss Hung. She quickly stepped up and got nose to nose with me.

"You American troglodyte!" she high whispered to my face. "I told you I couldn't do this, but *you* saw it necessary to do it anyway! We were just lucky that half the people watching convinced Mr. Sargent that *this* constitutes as a music video! Just to keep him happy I'm going to continue to run your video, but I'm telling you right now, you barf eater, if I'm called into his office over this, you can bet your over sized fanny that I'm going to implicate *you* too. And if that day comes I'm coming after you with a katana in hand to make sure you sing high soprano in the church choir! Do you read me?"

I didn't respond. She stormed away from me like she was ready to sprint just to leave my vicinity. To be honest, I thought she took my undercover espionage and sabotage better than I figured. Nonetheless, I felt my mission complete and she can do what she wants from here ...

It was about 1:30 Sunday afternoon, a few days after my video made it's debut in the Junior Miss Department. I was walking the self same circular wooden path checking the areas I clean for any last minute cleaning that needed to be done. As I approached the Junior Miss department I saw it was bustling with ... boys? They were all staring at the direction of the TVs and pointing at them. I rushed over to the area thinking that some disaster happened and I needed to call security. As I approached I saw the video of "Cosmic Relief" still playing on the screens and a group of boys watching it while moms and sisters comfortably shop the department. Usually boys are griping and moaning and whining for Mom and Sis to hurry up. Now all the boys are watching "Cosmic Relief" played on a Commodore 64. When Mom was ready to go it was the boys begging to stay in the department until such and such a scene was shown. Some moms were having to tear boys out of the Junior Miss department so they could shop somewhere else after Mom made a *big* purchase in the department. I walked close enough to the sales counter to overhear what the clerks were saying to each other:

"Gawd, so many people!" complained one, a tall, curly haired blonde. "You'd swear we were having a clearance sale."

"I know," said the brunette next to her. "All the boys are dragging their moms here just so they can watch this **** video!"

"I told my Mom about this video and the sales have picked up since we started playing it, and how they were working us extra to help out in making those sales and do you know what she said? 'Profit means paycheck and bigger profits means bigger paychecks!' What does she know? She's a housewife!"

I smiled. It seems like I have a hit on my hands, but I certainly didn't expect this: Boys telling Mom or Sis, "Why don't you shop longer? I'm good right here." Welcome to the world of the weird. I turned to go, but when I spun around to ended up nose to nose with Miss Hung again. Instead of breathing threats in my face she was actually smiling, her perfect pearl teeth reflecting the lights that illuminated the department. She took a step back, put her hands together, and bowed courteously to me.

"Domo arigato, Lenard san," she said to me. I raised an eyebrow. Is this the same woman who, a few days ago, was going to separate me from my family jewels and put them on display in a jar of formaldehyde? "Why do you waste your time as a custodian?" she asked. "You're excellent at generating sales. You should be a department manager. My sales have picked up about twenty five to thirty percent since your video debut. Boys are telling other boys about what we are showing on our TV and they are telling their mothers and sisters to shop *here* just so they can see the video. Christmas is coming soon. I can't wait to see what our sales margin will be like."

"What? And be denied all this?" I gestured at my uniform. "A wise man once said, 'Be content in whatever state ye are in.' I'm having fun, especially with my Commodore. That's where the video came from."

"I'm sorry I yelled at you," Miss Hung. "I didn't know at the time all this could happen."

"None of us have the gift of prophecy in this day and age," I said. "Leave that stuff to the Bible." I raised my hand. "Slap my hand?"

Miss Hung gave me a stinging high five. I shook my hand in pain. Miss Hung walked past me and giggled.

"Wimp," she said to me in a low voice.

Now, I told you that story to tell you this one ...

It was not too long after New Years 1990. I was just diagnosed with bipolar type 2 behavioral disorder, which made me quirky when I was on the job as custodian and Pickles Department Store. Management knew I was a possible danger to customers, employees, and myself, but I was good at my job and they didn't want to just "cut me loose" because I was mentally unstable, so they would see how I would perform under normal job pressures. This diagnosis didn't stop Miss Hung from conversing with me off and on during the course of a day. She sauntered up to me one day while I was making my circular rounds of her department with my trusty dust mop. She placed her hand on my shoulder.

"I heard you had another episode in cosmetics," she said softly. "Yeah," I answered. "This thing in my head won't give me any peace for very long. One small negative comment and BOOM! I have an instant mental meltdown. This is so not cool."

"What did Mr. Rogers say about it this time?" (Mr. Rogers is who we are going to call the General Manager of Pickles Department Store.)

"He understands that my psychiatrist is working as best that she can to find the right combination of medicines for me but he's going to have to let me go if this keeps up."

"Sounds like you could use a vacation," Miss Hung said with a quick smile.

"More like a distraction," I corrected. "Pushing a dust mop mindlessly through a department does not bode well for a bored mind."

I must have said something that triggered Miss Hung's mind for she quickly glanced away from me and her eyes moved to and fro like she was reading a cheap novel. After a few seconds of this odd behavior she lit up and looked square at me.

"I got just the thing," she said confidently. She took me by my wrist and led me to the Junior Miss Department where this whole thing began about six months ago. She made me stand in front of the three TVs in the department and left me there for a couple if moments. On screen, once again, came the video of "Cosmic Relief" that I made, but this show had blurs and static lines in the image. Miss Hung walked over and stood next to me; she gestured with her hand to the monitors.

"What's wrong with this picture?" she asked me.

I studied the images for a brief second. "Looks like the video is shot to Orion," I told her.

"Exactly," she said. "We burned this tape up quickly over the holidays by constantly playing it. You need a distraction? Make me another video."

"Do you want another video game?"

Miss Hung shook her head violently. "We got impossibly lucky last time and I don't want to tempt The Fates by trying to make lightning strike twice in the same place. Make me a music video."

Music video? On a Commodore 64? You mean with singers, guitars, drums, and the lot? How much crack does she smoke in a weekend? I'm a custodian not a magician! I asked Miss Hung for a couple of weeks to find and produce something knowing perfectly well in myself that I will have then what I have now -- zippo! She agreed and I left the department looking down at the floor.

"I'm going to need help with this project," I whispered to myself as I headed back to custodial storage with the dust mop in tow.

"... And that's the deal in a nutshell," I said to those in attendance of the Tuesday night meeting of the Commodore Users Group of Kansas City. "I need a music video that was produced using a Commodore computer."

"Can anyone help him out with this problem?" asked Diamond Frank, the CUGKC's president. The crowd of about fifteen users remained quiet. A squatty old man with more hair on his chin than he had on his head by a ratio of 2 to 1 spoke from the back of the meeting room.

"Let me see if I understand this correctly," he said in a calm yet commanding voice, "the program has to have music and a moving image, but it can't be a video game?"

"Correct, sir," I responded.

"Come see me after the meeting. I may be able to help."
After adjournment I walked by to the old man. As I drew closer I
saw that the individual looked like a cross between Santa Claus
and an Ewok. He was such a hairy person. I think he was trying to
make up for hair loss by beard growth. I didn't flinch but extended
my right hand out to him and introduced myself by my board
name, Captain L. He shook my hand with an extensive grip and
introduced himself as, "The Great Hairy One." He was a purveyor
of Commodore wares that was well known throughout the entire
four state area and beyond. If you had a specific hardware or
software need, chances were good to excellent that The Great
Hairy One would have it or know of someone who does.

"I think I have what you're looking for," he said in gruff but
pleasant voice. At his sales table, GHO had disk files broken down
into headings like "Productivity" and "Games," and some even
subdivided again into categories like "Sports" and "RPG" games.
On the edge of his table he had one disk file box marked "Music."
He opened it up and rifled through it quickly until he came to a
lone 5.25" disk that was hand labeled "Swinth". He handed it to
me.

"Load this into your computer and see if will fit what your job is
asking you of," he said. He also handed me his business card. "If
that won't work we'll try something else."

I gave GHO a five spot for the disk, dismissed myself from the
group, and quickly headed home with my treasure.

Summary of "Swinth" -- This is a psychedelic panorama of lights
and sound. The program lays down a line of color, followed by
another line until eight lines are laid down, then the first line on the
table is picked up and moved to the front, thus creating a moving

wave of lines with all the colors available on the Commodore cycle through. Combine this with melodic tunes from elsewhere on the program playing in the background and you can "go on a trip and never leave the house" type of scenario without the use of hypnotic stimulants or alcohol.

When I got home later that night I went right to my Commodore and booted the disk given me by GHQ. Just a few seconds of watching the computer generated image on screen brought a smile to my face. To quote Catwoman, "Purr-fect." I set the VCR up with my Commodore as I did before and took two hours out of my life to make a decent video. "I wonder how Miss Hung is going to like this?" I asked myself..

There were a few of the management staff as well as some of the sales help present in the Junior Miss department when my second video premiered on the monitors, including Dick Sargent himself. By now everyone knew that it was I and the Commodore 64 (someone in the department had loose lips) which produced the action packed game video of "Cosmic Relief" and they wanted to see of I was going to outdo myself. A few minutes into the music, color, and video display and everyone was convinced that this production was much better than the first. Dick was even enjoying the display and took the the time to thank Miss Hung for making the effort to improve her department sales and making Juniors and particularly Junior Miss the highest grossing sales department in the store for 1989.

"That's not all," Mr. Sargent continued, still addressing Miss Hung, "corporate in Little Rock were so impressed in your sales spike that they have asked me to honor you with the opportunity to become the new purchaser for all the Pickles stores from Houston to Minneapolis. Are you interested?"

Miss Hung didn't take long to think about it. "Yes!" she practically shouted. "Absolutely!"

"Excellent," Dick said with a smile. "There are a few details that has to be hammered out in Mr. Rogers' office. You'll be sent to Little Rock in two weeks to start training. Let me be the first to say, 'Congratulations.'"

Dick gently shook Miss Hung's hand. Loyal sales clerks and other department managers hugged on her and gave their congratulations as well. It was a quick, spontaneous party that broke out in the Junior Miss Department while"Swinth" for the Commodore 64 played melodically in the background. I didn't want to be hanging around all this estrogen charged emotionalism so I found a quick way out of the crowd and headed back to the custodial room to grab my lunch box and go home to feed my cats. No sooner than my clipping my lunchbox shut the loud thud of the double doors leading to the custodial area could be heard. I spun around with lunchbox in hand wanting to know who just about busted the doors off the hinges.

"And where the h*ll do you think you're going?" You guessed it; it was Miss Hung.

I pointed at my watch. "It's almost 2 pm. Time for me to go home."

She stormed up to me and put her hands on her hips. She tried to look stern at me with disgruntled determination, but her arms went to her side and her face fell. I think I saw tears well up in her eyes, too.

"Why?" she asked. "I didn't like you, you're disgusting, you hardly ever shave, you smell like a mix of deodorant and Drano, and I did everything I knew including talking to Mr. Sargent about getting

119

another custodian to take over cleaning my department because you're just gross. I tried to make your life as miserable as possible down here so you would quit, but you decided to do all this -- and I mean those crazy videos -- for me, despite my objections. Why?" I set my lunchbox back on the table, looked at the tips of my shoes, and breathed deeply. I didn't know what to tell her right off, but what came out of my mouth surprised even me: "I think that if Jesus owned a Commodore, He would have done the same thing for you, too."

I raised my hand for another high five, but Miss Hung threw her arms around my neck, and squeezed. She started crying softly into my chest bone and her hug popped a couple of vertebrae in my neck.

"Thank you, you dirty, smelly, rotten old man," Miss Hung said through her tears. "Thanks for everything."

She let go of me and watched as I climbed into the freight elevator that would take me to the second floor. I had to admit, I was getting high off the pheromones and her perfume was a pleasing aphrodisiac, but I couldn't take advantage of the apparent situation. That would make me a "creep" and she and I would never be the same. However, I did have to stop in at the men's restroom and soak my head in the sink with cold water before I could hit the time clock. I may have been old but I certainly wasn't dead.

EPILOGUE --

The "Swinth" Commodore music video took off just as well as the "Cosmic Relief" video game did, but with a much older crowd. One sales clerk made a copy of the tape and showed it to her husband, who used the music and images to help him down stress and meditate after a hard day at the office. This seemed to make him a more attentive and responsible man at home. Sadly,

"Swinth" brought out a dark side in some as well as they would take a copy of the video and watch it at home after taking a big hit of acid. Apparently, such a drug brought out the sound and color of the video to the viewer.

Miss Hung was replaced by a stout, by the book brunette who would not deviate to the left or the right when it came to company policy. A sales clerk took the master copy of "Swinth" home and it was never seen again.

As for me, I had that final violent manic episode that got me dismissed from Pickles Department Store, but I went out in a blaze of glory. I injured three of the city's finest before they all ganged up on me, slammed me onto a table, cuffed me, and hauled me to the hospital's psychiatric department where I stayed for a month. A tragic end to an otherwise triumphant tale of Commodore know how...

Shift-Clr/Home

TITLE: If Wisdom Wore Tennis Shoes

POINT OF ORIGIN: Reset Magazine

MODE: Essay or commentary

SYNOPSIS: In this essay, Lenard looks at his dream of being a stay at home programmer gets set aflame and how, out of the ashes, a brighter Phoenix arises than he never saw coming. Thought provoking.

Shift-Clr/Home

If Wisdom Wore Tennis Shoes (And Other Natural Flavors)

As I sat back in my office chair, I stared at the Commodore 128 that was before me and thought, "What infinite possibilities have been given to us who live in the Free World, with just the simple design and construction of such a machine." When you think about it, after thirty years since it's release in the very early 80s, the Commodore computer still has new and innovative software and hardware coming out for it. I don't think a month has gone by without some ingenious person coming out with something new. I still lay in bed once in a while and try to think of either what I can write in the way of new software or re-code an already existing piece of software.

There was a time back in the early 90s that I honestly thought I could stop working outside my little shanty in urban Kansas City, Kansas (aka: God's Country) and do nothing but sit at home in my underwear and code programs for the Commodore. This was an adventurous idea that was fueled by my first successful sale of a 26-block program called "Check It Out" to a nation wide Commodore magazine. Yeah, I was thinking, "Three or four programs a month, sell them to a magazine will more than pay the bills, put groceries in the pantry, and put some aside in savings, will more than suffice this dude!" I should have known that "Providence suffereth him not to live" as my main source of a purchaser of new Commodore software went dry the very next month and with it my hopes of being an independent writer and coder for the machine. Thankfully I was wise enough at the time to not quit work so I went back to the 6 am to 2 pm bump and grind with no loss of pay, but with the loss of a dream.

Moving forward from '92 to now, it seems that, despite the fact that Commodore is no longer mainstream, it still seems to slowly grow in popularity again. Some of this generation's gaming community want to step back in time and play some of the 80s style of video games that were indigenous to the Commodore, and even some gamers were adventurous enough to get the actual hardware and software to run these games to get the entire "retro" feeling. I sometimes think it's silly to be fifty plus years old and still play video games on occasion, but I'm from the era when video games were first introduced. Everything that the modern day gamer has got its nucleus from games and coders like me. Now I have to admit that my kind of programming revolves around more of productivity software right now with my personal fascination with budgeting and finance, so any "luxury" programming like games and video puzzles escape me, but before I get to that state where the ground hogs deliver your mail I'd like to learn "freestyle" Commodore game programming. As I have said in many different articles in the past, I have a small collection of game "construction sets" where all the user does is enter bits of information and the program does the coding for you. I think the downfall of such software is the user could not sell his pre-packaged creation to a software company because the coding mechanics was already copyrighted, thus making whatever the programmer made an instant ownership of the corporation holding said copyright. Here in the 21st century, Commodore users still using pre-packaged game coding software may not give a feline's flatulence about copyrights, but simply want to have fun on the Commodore. Rumors have reached this Ancient One's ears that today's retro programmer's are using Commodore emulators on the laptop or PC to code and taking the finished product out of emulation and either putting it on disk or directly uploading the image to the Internet. I've tried doing that with my Commodore word processing and the felgercarbing emulator crashed and I lost half a manuscript that I battled to write and finish, with no hardcopy or soft copy backups. Retard! So, I must stand in a very old schoolhouse where only real Commodore machines are the best for doing Commodore work; emulators can bite the big red potato!

Where is Commodore going? There's a question to ponder. With the creation of better and faster PCs there comes the destruction of the old to make way for the new. Commodore also fell this way when it's processor became too slow and the memory inefficient to keep up with the demands of the times. But someone, or a group of someones, must have decided that this aging 8-bit still had capabilities that would make it useful in the 21st century and beyond. All one had to do was increase on board memory capacity and a faster processor. This innovation came to fruition as accelerators, attachments, and internal upgrades made it possible for the Commodore, who at one time was the big dog, to keep up (though taking up the rear) with demands for more onboard space and a rapid processors.

What about stock units? Are they still viable in such a fast paced world? As a user of stock Commodore computers I can tell you, "Yes they are." All of my article writing and coding are done primarily on the Commodore 128 with no Jiffy DOS or other speed and memory enhancements. As for extra on board memory I still use good old fashioned 5.25 DSDD disks that still are holding up after all these decades. I find it quite an accomplishment when some of my writings fill both sides of a disk and I get to move on to the next one. When I run out of 5.25s to fill I have some beat up 3.5s that can hold a byte or two.

With all this written down on paper (or whatever medium you prefer) it still comes down to the out and out fact that the Commodore brand of computers are just plain fun to work with. I don't think that since the invention of the automobile has one such machine has had a bonding effect on the end user. Commodore was made to help man achieve greatness and help him in life while today's PC more or less tells man what to do and how to do it, which means the coder sitting in the cubicle at some IT conglomerate in a remote part of the earth really runs the world, and what's really scary is ... I think that they know it.

To finish up this prattling of a Mid Western redneck, I want to leave you with a thought to ponder: The enemies of the Free World supposedly have some sort of computer dampening device that, when activated, is suppose to scramble all the data in large mainframes and hard drives, making them useless, thereby virtually crippling, if not totally shutting down, governments, military, and big business that relies heavily on technology. If this conspiracy theory is true, where will this leave the Commodore? My guess is that it will leave Commodore out front as the only computer around that doesn't rely heavily on such support, but Commodore, with its stand alone capacity and it's storage on removable mediums, will become the computer of need in such an apocalyptic digital nightmare.

Thanks for reading this column during your time with your morning coffee, afternoon tea, or evening brew. I look forward to sitting across the table with you again and discussing with you all items that are Commodore. Next time we meet I hope to share with you my method on how I prepare myself to write such interesting (?) prattle.

TITLE: Let The Magic Begin Anew

POINT OF ORIGIN: Reset Magazine

MODE: Story

SYNOPSIS: Lenard takes a point in his life and re tells the tale embellishing a Commodore into the mix wherein the machine is used to help him treat his bipolarism.

Shift-Clr/Home

Let The Magic Begin Anew
(Commodore fiction based on real events)

The physicians met behind closed doors while I waited outside on the sofa, wondering what they were talking about. I could only imagine what the conversation was going like –

"I don't know what to do with Mr. Roach," one doctor might say. "We've tried just about every medicine on the planet and nothing seems to help him."

"If it wasn't for his insurance being so well packaged, I would have sent him home long ago and let him live out his life there with this condition running through his mind," another might say.

"Let his family deal with him!" a third might exclaim.

One doctor, probably the one who attended me most during my stay in the psyche ward, may have stood up in front of his fellow physicians and said, "People, maybe we are approaching Mr. Roach's bipolarism from the wrong direction. We are trying to shove a drug store down his neck; maybe there's a therapy we haven't tried yet."

"Perhaps, but which one?" a voice would ask from the far end of the table.

That's when she rolled in. She was an elderly lady, stricken to a wheelchair for some years by a debilitating disease that I don't know about. Her hair was cut short and powdered with white and black strands. Her features made her look like a strong stage actor whose presence would draw applause for her just showing up. She was thin and not well built. There was nothing about the woman that would attract any suitor, but she wasn't interested in dating; she was interested in healing the sick.

131

She rolled up to the table with all these educated people staring at her, not to stare at her handicap, but because they knew that if any had any suggestions to help me, it was her. She may have stopped her chair just short of the doctor sitting at the head of the table. She may even have tried to stare down the others who were there, but all focused their attention on her.

"Give Mr. Roach to me," she might have said. "I think I may have a solution."

Without any hesitation, the physicians pointed me out, sitting just outside the door. She wheeled herself out the main door and into the psyche ward waiting room where I sat. She came up to me, smiled, and took my hand.

"Are you ready to try something different?" she asked me.

"I'm tired of medications," I responded, "nothing seems to work with me."

"This isn't medication, this will be therapy. Something I think will help you."

"I'll try anything," I said, "just make me think like a person again."

"Then meet me in the patient lounge at 10:30 and we'll begin with the other students in the group."

At 10:30, I walked into the patient's lounge and there sitting with the woman in the wheelchair was a group of folk who seemed to have it together. They communicated with each other intelligently; they laughed and smiled and none of it seemed like their facial expressions were psychotic or unreal; they were – human. On their laps were clipboards with paper and in their hands were pens and pencils. I was ushered into the room by a gesture from the woman.

She pointed to a funny looking device that I would later discover was called a keyboard, a disk drive, and a monitor.

"I understand from your profile that you can type pretty good," she said. "This is a typewriter of sorts. It's a word processing program loaded from a disk in that disk drive into what is known as a Commodore 64. This will be your instrument to use during our sessions. No one else has the privilege to use this unit but you. I'll show you how to load and run the software later; right now it's ready to go. Don't worry about the semantics of the program, just do what I tell you and the rest of the class."

I sat down at the funny thing which seemed to have more wires running to and from it than my dad's old 67 Bel Air station wagon, but I saw on the keyboard that the keys were arranged just like they were on a standard typewriter. I poised my fingers on the keys like a concert pianist ready to give the performance of a lifetime, and waited.

When the woman in the wheelchair saw I was ready, she turned to the rest and spoke. "Now students, I want all of you to start writing about the time when you felt the most betrayed. Be as detailed or a vague as you want; make your statement as long or as short as you want, just get your feelings out on paper. Go."

With the ten or so people in that room, each of them scratching with a pen or pencil, it sounded like a cat digging into the cat litter covering its latest deposit. The sounds I made were completely different – ticka, ticka, ticka -- as I started out slowly trying to get the feel of this non-typewriter typewriter, but soon the emotions started to flow as I thought about when I was hurt the most. I typed faster and faster as the moment came back to me in full review, but the faster I typed, the more mistakes I made. I found the delete key and backed up several times, each time breaking my stride on the emotional tidal wave.

"Don't worry about mistakes in your writing," the woman in the wheelchair explained as she came up behind me, "just keep going and don't let that moment escape you. Write it all down; every second, every emotion, every action. Don't correct anything, just keep going."

With great fervor I pounded on that poor Commodore 64. I was getting so fast that really thought that for a minute I was Clark Kent at the Daily Planet beating Lois Lane on a story, with me having the power to type 5,000 words a minute. Before I knew it the hour for the session was up. Many of the patients were done and milling about the lounge, some were still working on the assignment like me, but they only had paper and pencil or pen, while I had the help of the Commodore 64 word processor, I had more done, but even after the session was over I was still typing. The woman put her hand on my shoulder.

"You can stop now, Lenard," she said. "You've done enough for today. We'll pick this up again tomorrow."

I got up from the chair and the Commodore 64 and she rolled herself into my place. With a few clicks of the keys, the disk drive roared into action with red and green lights flashing like it was Christmas morning. After a few seconds the drive settled down. She lifted a lever in the front of the disk drive and out popped a flat, square plastic plate with a hole in it dead center. She turned her chair around to face me.

"I've saved all that you've written onto this disk," she explained, "and I'll read what you have written on my own Commodore 64 at home. Go have some lunch, but before you go, tell me, how do you feel now?"

I never thought about my emotions for the hour I was on the Commodore 64. I was pouring all my emotions into the

Commodore there in the lounge, spelling out every emotion and feeling that I could think of, and not thinking of anything else, but for the first time in a while my thoughts weren't running 100 miles an hour, thinking of hurting anyone else or killing myself. For the first time in many months –

"I feel...great," I told her. "I feel calm, collected, in control; I haven't felt like this in months." I looked at her with amazement. "How did you do it?"

She chuckled a little, then looked into my eyes with her own blue eyes. "Me? I didn't do a thing. You did it all yourself. You've always had the capacity to help yourself, Lenard, you just needed someone to point you into the right direction, and I think, by golly, that we may have found that direction."

For the remaining two weeks I was in the psychiatric ward at the hospital, I looked forward to 10:30 and the little woman in the wheelchair who seemed to have the power to open my soul on a Commodore 64's word processor. She even taught me some basic Commodore commands so I could load the word processor and save my work to that very same disk she took home every day. The students (I was surprised she never called us "patients" but "students") and myself were always working on something different every day for those two weeks, never taking a day off; we even attended on weekends. It was the best stay I've ever had in a psyche ward.

Two weeks later I was sitting on the same sofa, but this time with my bag packed and ready to go home to my wife and children, but there was still one more behind closed doors meeting that the doctors had to have concerning me, this time with the little woman in the wheelchair attending, sitting at the head of the table. I could only imagine what they might be saying now.

"I don't know how you did it, doctor," the head physician in charge of my case might say, "but Mr. Roach has made a complete 180 and is ready to go home. What in God's name did you do?"

I'm sure she gave him and the rest of the attendees a brief but direct explanation of what she did, my "treatment," as it were, and how that, with less medication, I was able to function again with the rest of society. The head doctor, I'm sure, leaned back in his chair with a big smile on his face.

"Good work, doctor," he might say. "Mr. Roach is discharged and ready to go home." The head physician would look at the attending nurse next to him. "Please give Mr. Roach his list of medications to take before he goes home."

"Right away, doctor," she would respond and exit the board room. All the doctors left at once, with the woman in the wheelchair coming out last. She rolled herself over to me on the sofa.

"You're free to go."

"What will I do now?" I asked. "What's my next form of treatment?"

"You'll be visiting a therapist for the next several months. The nurse will be bringing you a list of medications that you need to go to the pharmacy and fill." She put her hand on my shoulder again. "And never, ever, ever, stop writing. Put your feelings down on paper or computer every day. You've got some talent there, Lenard. I'm not surprised that you'll be a successful author someday."

I looked down at my hands. "I never thought of that before," I told her, "but you've opened a whole new world for me. I don't know how to thank you."

She chuckled again. "You can thank me by going out there, live your life, and never let me see you back in this facility again."

"I'll try."

"Yoda said, 'Do, or do not. There is no try.'"

"Yes, doctor. Thanks for being here. Good luck and God bless you and your work."

The nurse came out of her station and gave me my list of medications to take.

"Watching people like you walk out of this facility a lot better off than when they came in, I think He already has."

I grabbed my bag, stood up, and waited for security to open the door to the outside.

"One more thing, Lenard, " the lady in the wheelchair said, "you're wife and kids have a surprise for you when you get home."

"What is it?" I asked.

"If I told you then it wouldn't be a surprise."

She laughed as security opened the door and escorted me to the waiting cab.

My wife threw her arms around me and squeezed the dickens out of me when I walked into the house a new man, a new husband, and a new father. Behind her were my friends who took care of my family while I was in the hospital. They all shook my hand and mussed up my hair as I stood there with my family.

"The doctor said that you have a surprise waiting for me."

My wife and friends spread out like Moses opening the Red Sea and allowed me to see, sitting in the living room, an exact copy of the Commodore 64 that I used while I was in the hospital, complete with disk drive and a printer. I walked slowly over the machine and lightly touched its keys, remembering the unit that was in the patient's lounge at the hospital. I looked over the disk drive and printer like a archaeologist checking a rare artifact. I glanced back at my wife.

"The doctor said you could use one of these," she said with a smile. "It's a hand me down, but it still works."

My friends rolled an office chair up to the Commodore 64 and invited me to take a seat. I sat down at the machine and looked into the monitor, where the same word processor I was using at the hospital was loaded and the cursor was flashing, waiting for input. I looked around at everyone with a tear in my eye, then looked back at the Commodore. I poised my fingers on the keyboard as I have done for two weeks before.

Let me magic begin anew …

TITLE: Fruit Loops And Corn Dogs

POINT OF ORIGIN: Reset Magazine

MODE: Story essay

SYNOPSIS: Lenard tells the story of how he got started writing for Commodore newsletters and magazines instead of just being another faceless user. He also gives some advice for those wanting to write. Fun and heartwarming.

Shift-Clr/Home

Fruit Loops And Corn Dogs
(With A Little Advice Thrown In For Irritation)

People have emailed, called, or come up to me in person and asked, "Pops, how do you come up with things to say about the Commodore line of computers after all this time?"

How does anyone write anything about anything? You have to sit down with what you are doing and study it. I've been writing off and on about Commodores since 1995 when I was first asked by Diamond, then the president of The Commodore Users Group of Kansas City to describe in an article style format about what a visitor to my BBS, "The Pulpit", would find. I said, "Sure. Why not?" I wrote the article in precise detail, throwing in commentary on each subboard. My command of the Queen's English (and my own redneck slur) was rusty, but despite that I put a lot of heart into the piece and, when done, it was sent to the editor of the club's newsletter, "Ryte Bytes". What went in was, what I thought, a masterpiece of literary art; what reached final publication turned out to be a chopped down form that, to the editor, was more "reader friendly." The problem? "The Pulpit" was a religious BBS, which may prove to be "offensive" to some of our readers.

Offensive?! What he did to my article was offensive to *me!* Did he ever think of that? I took my free copy of the newsletter (my "fee" for being a contributor), and sat down for the meeting to begin, my ego severely bruised, beaten, and knocked down but not destroyed. I sat there the whole meeting licking my wounds. This was it. No more for me.

Next month Diamond approached me again to ask a favor:

"Lenard, you program in BASIC, right?"

"A little." Three years ago I got a $150 check in the mail from

"Run" magazine for a program called "Check It Out" and Diamond knew that so yeah, I do a "little" programming.

"Are you working on anything right now?" Diamond asked.

"I'm farting around with a couple of projects." What was he driving at?

"Can you write a column in the newsletter each month about what you're working on and your progress? It might prove of interest to our readers."

I glared at Diamond and told him rather vividly and very brashly of what the editor did to my last piece. Diamond apologized.

"That was my fault," he confessed. "I didn't know your BBS was on a controversial subject. Just write one article about what you've been working on and submit it. I'll look at it with the editor and we'll decide together how to handle it."

I was apprehensive, but with the person wanting my submission and the guy trying to butcher what I write working together something might come out of it. I went home that night and looked over a project I was working on. I wrote in detail on what the program was suppose to do, what hurdles I had to jump, problems I was looking at and possible solutions. I drafted the piece, polished it, and sent it in. The article came out at the next meeting with nary a word changed. This was a surprise! I was sure that the editor would proverbially emasculate my writings again, but there it was almost word for word. The reason? "You put nothing in this article that was controversial. You talked about programming and kept God out of it. It flew."

Sometimes you have the choice of doing what you want over doing what you know to be right. The Bible calls this a "passing pleasure." Yeah, even though I knew better, I enjoyed the accolades of men over the accolades of God. So for next eight years I wrote fantastic articles about whatever I could find that would associate with the Commodore computer: My cat and the Commodore, my dog and the Commodore, my kids and the Commodore, flatulence and the Commodore, taking the Commodore to work, taking the Commodore to church, buying Commodores, selling Commodores, and on and on. The articles ideas came flowing so fast that I had to start my own newsletter in 2000 that ran for two years just to get all the ideas out on paper. "The Secret Organization of Commodore Users" it was called, and it was met with praise and a slap of the hand both at the same time. Some big Commodore clubs didn't want anything to do with SOOCU because it didn't appeal to the advance user; smaller clubs appreciated the fresh ideas and good natured writing, but cost and time became a factor so I dropped the project. My most famous and still the most reproduced article was my story of two of my cats attacking my Commodore stand in the middle of night. It was entitled "Raiders At Midnight." Those animals who starred in that article have long since gone to pet heaven.

In 2006 or thereabouts, the CUGKC, with me as it's last president, shut it's doors after a vote from it's presiding membership, so there I sat from 2006 to 2010 with no outlet for my Commodore programs and articles. I decided to mess around on the Commodore anyway and basically code programs that I saw I needed for myself to make life easier at the house. I might even try my hand at game coding. From those short years I didn't master much, and nothing I coded was worth the disk I saved it on.

I'm getting my timeline mixed up here for somewhere along the line I sent a query letter to Mr. Moorman of Loadstar over "The Envelope Addressor" and his publication shot me quickly back up into the eyes of the Commodore public. I remember the CUGKC critiquing the work in Loadstar thus promoting me to code another version of it called "TEA 4.2". I also know my son Calibur went through his battle with leukemia (and won) and that was in 2004. I also remember 100% self publishing my first Commodore book, "Run/Stop-Restore" in 2000 which only sold two whole copies. I met Robert Bernardo and the Fresno (California) Commodore User Group and became a long distance member. I quickly became the club's newsletter editor of which I still occupy that post as of this writing. I know that in August 2010, my wife of 26 years divorced me to marry the man she was having an affair with. After this, in December 2010, I re-released my first book with some new writings and essays on the Commodore and re-titled it, "Run/Stop-Restore: 10th Anniversary Edition" using Author House of Springfield, Illinois as my publisher, and, with new contacts from FCUG and "The Village Green" (Astoria, Oregon), this book was widely accepted and continues to sell copies as of this writing.

Let me be honest, the people of Commodore were some of the high elite of folk that really assisted me in the years of healing from a devastating divorce as everyone read my material and were nice enough to contact me and thank me for writing that piece, or they didn't see that Commodore function, or that Commodore command in that way. Did my church family help? You bet! They, like the people of Commodore, loved me to death while I was dying inside. After this, I realized that, even though I kind of "phased" God out of my work on Commodore, that crazy, four goose bozo Heavenly Father was right in the middle of my entire Commodore endeavors and escapades, gently prodding me on towards the future building of my skills as a Commodore writer, commentator, and coder.

So, to answer the question first posed at the beginning of this article, all I can suggest is that, if you want to write for Commodore you must sit down and just -- do it! Don't know where to start? Don't punish yourself. The first sentence is hardest to write, but put something down either on paper or in a word processor. One phrase I read in a Commodore magazine once was about a free type in program to turn your Commodore into a precursor of today's Kindle e-book called, "It Was A Dark And Stormy Night ..." Try that title for a start. There's also, "It's funny to me when ..." or "While using my Commodore one day I noticed ..." The universe is your tablet and the Commodore is your premise. Please remember something my writing teacher, Ms. Enell, taught me: "Everything is publishable and worthy to be read by someone."

Now a word about critics, and you *will* have at least one or two, trust me. A wise pastor and author once said to his congregation about this subject, "Everyone who puts words to paper will receive criticism. You cannot avoid it. If you can't handle the criticism then get out of the writing business. It's not for you. You've got to have a thick enough hide to take the chewing and gnawing that a critic will do to you, your work, your family, and your lifestyle. The best way to toughen your hide to deal with a critic is to just let them rant. Chances are likely they are trying to build for themselves a reputation and they want to use the rubble they try to tear you down into as a stepping stone." When it comes down to the point where you must answer a critic, don't react emotionally or without thinking, first and foremost. Use a medium you are best familiar with, like, for me, it's the printed word. Be short and precise. Try to give them as little ammunition from your stockpile of supplies as possible. Let them shoot off their mouth as much as they can. A wise saying from my bygone days is: "A person is considered wise until he opens his mouth and removes all doubt." Summary: Ignore critics and move on to your next subject.

This reminds me of my first story I ever submitted to "Reset." I wrote a rant about Commodores being permanently put to the wayside and even girlfriends are asking their men to end the "love affair" with our machine of choice. "Uncle K" was nice enough to print it up in "Reset," and he got a critic's response to it in his "Letters To The Editor" email. He forwarded it to me asking to respond to this reader. The critic asked me, "What cave do I live in?" and proceeded to give his personal examples to my "flawed" reasoning about Commodore's stand in the dedicated user's household. My first response? You guessed it: Nyet. In fact, I got about half way through a soon-to-be new submission and even scribbled out a couple of skits for some local church clients before I sat down and studied the critic's note. I read and re-read the letter until my eyeballs bled. I knew that whatever I said to this person was only going to start a whole new firestorm. I don't remember what I told the reader but "Uncle K" said my response took up 1 1/2 pages in the next issue. He also forwarded my response to his letter to the critic and he sent another 1 1/2 pages back. "Uncle K" said that, between the reader and myself, we could possibly fill a whole issue of "Reset" with our tete a tete, so "Uncle K" made a wise decision and dropped the letter and my response. The reader was articulate, well mannered, intelligent, and well versed in the Queen's English. I have to confess that when it comes to a battle of wits, I am an unarmed man.

Please don't feel like I'm trying to deter you from writing about Commodore and putting it in the pages of "Reset", your local club newsletter, or anywhere else; I just want you to know what you may go through in doing so.

TITLE: The Commodore Jedi Master

POINT OF ORIGIN: Reset Magazine

MODE: Biography

SYNOPSIS: Lenard's best friend, Commodore trainer, and sage, Carl, is remembered and eulogized in this piece that needing special permission from his widow before it went to press. Pictures were included in the original publication that were not included in this reprint.

Shift-Clr/Home

The Commodore Jedi Master

(Written with the expressed consent from The Estate of Carl B. Zuel)

Everyone who uses a Commodore had someone who introduced them to the machine. Maybe your person was the quick talking enthusiastic sales clerk in the electronics department in your local mall. Maybe yours was the kind, elderly relative who thought you might enjoy this Commodore thingamabob for Christmas so it ended up under your tree. Me? It was the gift of a used Commodore 64, printer, and tape drive from my wife's best friend at the time, but I am getting ahead of myself. For this to be a true tale of Commodore glory we must turn the hands of time back even further to when Commodore first hit the market in my little burg of what would soon grow into the city of Olathe.

Carl and I went to the same high school. He was a sophomore and I was a senior. Back then I was big into superhero comics and I brought a bunch to a dress rehearsal of a play we were both starring in and he started thumbing through the issues. I said something stupid to him and we hit it off instantly. Before I knew it we were going to midtown Kansas City every Saturday at 10 am to make our weekly "comic book run" to a little shop at 40th and Main.

One Christmas Day Carl showed me an interesting device his parents got him that was on sale at Sears Roebuck for $600. I went with him into his room and he showed me what I ignorantly called a "typewriter". He corrected me by explaining that it was a personal computer called a Commodore 64. It was the high tech, top of the line gadget available on the market. He told me about all things it could do: It could be a typewriter, it could be a video game, it can talk on the telephone, it can even be told what it can become by simply typing on the keyboard certain key phrases called BASIC. He showed me a few functions; he even let me sit down at the machine and play with it. I was mesmerized! I couldn't wait to get home and tell my new wife that we needed a Commodore 64 in the house. At home, the wife heard of Carl's gift and instantly shot down my hopes and aspirations of getting a system of our own. "$600 just isn't in the budget," she explained. I was heartbroken but I knew she was right. I had a baby to feed and bills to pay before I got something as nifty as a Commodore 64. That was 1984.

Coming to Christmas 1988, I got a slightly used Commodore 64 for Christmas. I was goat hopping crazy happy when I got it and instantly called Carl in Olathe (I was married with one son and living in Kansas City, Kansas by this time) and told him that I finally got a unit of my own. I couldn't wait to start working on writing my movie script that has been stuck in my head for months.

"Hold it a minute, Lenard," Carl said over my receiver, "you'll need proper software to change the computer into a word processor. Come to my fraternity house at the college after classes resume and I'll fix you up." (Carl was attending Wichita State University by this time and was home for holiday). Right after New Years 1989 I climbed into the Chevette and made the four hour drive to Wichita, Kansas and to the Kappa Sigma fraternity house where Carl was a member. Carl was already a Big Man on Campus since he was the only person in any fraternity house to have a personal computer. I went to his room where he had his Commodore 128 set up. (He apparently upgraded). A quick scan of the local boards and he found me the perfect word processing package that would work best with the Commodore 64 and my tape drive, "Speedscript 3.0" from "Compute Gazette" magazine. Carl happened to have that issue where the word processor was printed and gave it to me to use as a user manual. I thanked him and, after dinner, I headed back to Kansas City with the program neatly tucked into a cassette. I wrote my first and only movie, "Crimebusters," on that Commodore 64 using the tape drive and 30 minutes of a 60 minute cassette.

With that magazine that Carl let me borrow were other programs written in BASIC, BASIC machine, and machine language, and I started to study how this type of talking worked with the Commodore. Before long most of the algebra I learned in high school started to come back to mind and programming started to make sense, especially BASIC. Before long I was writing short subroutines which, I hoped, I could use later.

In spring 1992, I was in my car heading again to see Carl at Wichita State. I just coded my very first salable program for the Commodore 64, but it lacked definition when it came to printing. I sent the program several times over to Carl using the GEnie network and Carl couldn't do anything with it; he had to see the actual working model. By late morning I again stood in Carl's room at the Kappa Sigma fraternity house watching him muse over what I wrote.

"It's good, man," he said, "and I'm sure a magazine will pick it up, but let me add a tweak that will make it more user friendly."

Carl booted the program and within five minutes was already saving a final copy. The problem I had was calculating how many dashes (-) should go behind the printed amount on the amount line of a check. Carl set up a few algebraic expressions that told the Commodore to figure it out and print needed dashes onto the check. It worked brilliantly when I got it home. Carl also eliminated my SYS64738 command saying to me that the program will now work on a Commodore 128 in 40 column mode with that BASIC expression gone, and sure enough, it did. I promised him $100 of my sales to him, expecting to get $1,000 from any magazine since this program was so necessary to life in the early

1990s. He told me to forget it or give it to a charity.

I saw Carl twice after this meeting: Once, when he married his high school sweetheart Juli and a second time a couple of years later to buy his Commodore 128 for he was leaving the Commodore world to operate the growing IBM world.

My best friend ever died of a blood clot in November 1998 at the very young age of 33 -- the same age Jesus Christ was when He was nailed to a coarse wooden Roman cross. Parallel universe.

Carl imparted much wisdom to me, especially in the new field of computing that he and I both explored. I've compiled a few things he told me to do especially when working on the Commodore. I hope in the remainder of this article to share with you, the reader, what Carl, the Commodore Jedi master, shared with me, the Commodore padawan:

"Save early and save often" -- This was at the top of Carl's list of functions to do when he himself was coding on the Commodore. As with even today's computers a person must save the work early and often. You *never* know when any computer will crash so be sure that as little data as possible ends up accidentally going into the Abyss of the Unknown.

"Save under a different file name" -- Carl believed that when you progress, subroutine by subroutine, in your coding adventure, save your work, yes, but save the work into several different file names. Carl suggested using numbers in a sequence like: PROGRAM1, PROGRAM2, and etc. Why? He said that you may write a subroutine that doesn't fit well with the whole program, but it may work in a future work. Also, if there is a hiccup that is created and added to the work in progress, you can delete or note the offending subroutine and have the previous functioning code safely saved beforehand.

"Always checksum" -- Carl gave me this advice back when Commodore was just starting to lose status with the computing masses. When I coded "Check It Out" I check summed the work to death. The program without checksums was about 20 blocks in size; with checksums added it was about 33 blocks. If it wasn't for a Commodore function called "crunching" I would never been able to bring the program down to the workable size of 26 blocks. This was also the maximum block size allowed by "Run" magazine for publishing. Carl taught me to crunch also, which I do a lot whether the program needs it or not, but checksums, well, I have to confess I don't add too many of those to my newer Commodore works because they are cumbersome to write and, I hope, the 21st century Commodore user is a little bit smarter than what they were in the 80s and 90s. If any mistakes happen during input by the user in any of my programs, I try to provide an out which usually requires the poor user to re-input all the information from start point alpha. Sorry Master Z, I have broken a sacred commandment. Your forgiveness I implore.

"Make multiple copies on several disks" -- Carl, as I stated before, believed in "save early; save often." He also believed in the above statement. One too many times he lost important files, documents, and programs to the evils of disk integrity failure. Even with fresh 5 1/4" disks from the computer store he would still lose data to the sin of lax manufacturing of DSDD disks. Carl always preached to use direct from Commodore hardware and software products. Carl imbedded in me the desire of making multiple copies of my Commodore work onto several disks. When Carl changed platforms due to necessity and sold me his Commodore 128, he kept back a few disks not for personal use, but they had personal information on them that I should not see. I suspect there were love letters to his wife on those disks that were meant "for her eyes only." Everyone has secrets. I respect his decision.

Carl said more than this, but my ancient memory can't recall these quotes right at this scripting. He was a friend, brother, and teacher to me and, I suspect, to others as well. More than his family and friends lost a great man, but the Commodore world lost a great coder and educator. God bless you, Master Z. God bless yours. Goodbye, farewell, and amen...

TITLE: What Else Can Be Said?

POINT OF ORIGIN: Reset Magazine

MODE: Commentary

SYNOPSIS: Lenard tells of all the various writing tools that he has access to and uses, but concludes that nothing is better than the old standby of the Commodore computer

Shift-Clr/Home

What Else Can Be Said?

Technicians, hardware gurus, and every day people have been talking, writing, and demonstrating items about the Commodore computer for over thirty years, and there's *still* more to be said about the machine. You would figure that all that can be said has been said, but no. As long as there are die hard Commodore retro users out there (I think I heard a report once of there being a little over one million world wide) there will always something to be said about the machine.

When I get my issue of "Reset" downloaded from the website the first place I go to is my article. I'm always curious as to what the editor has done with the piece. I'm also interested as to where in the magazine my article is placed. I'm usually blessed to have a location about midway through. As a person who uses writing more for the therapy than actually having something to say, I'm grateful that magazines and newsletters actually think that these ramblings are worth putting into print. My writing instructor has taught me that *everything* is worthy of print, even some private writings so make sure if you don't want something read, you burn it to a crackly crunch. I expect my children to make my journals public after I pass from this world so people can meet the hidden me.

Most everyone who reads my columns in "Reset" know well what I do with the Commodore as it is my retro gaming device, my word processor, my program creation center, and my budgeting device. I try to do as much as I can on my Commodore but working three "start up" jobs just to pay the bills and stock the cupboards with food takes up much of my time. I needed to find a way to write when I'm on break as a convenience store clerk, waiting for an order as a courier, or resting between floors as a custodian. I was looking in the world of Commodore for help but there was nothing but the bulky SX64 sitting in the computer room. Though portable it is hardly convenient. I had to turn to other devices that can provide me with word processing power, be smaller than an SX64, and portable.

I went to my stack of old cellphones. Most of these have word processors built in or can be downloaded through a wifi connection so re-activating them to a wireless network would be unnecessary. Then I found what I was looking for sitting in that stack; the old iPhone 4. I remember using this phone to make notes on its Notes application when I used to drive people to the airport (another failing job I had). Notes for iPhone works similar to Notepad in Windows. It is a "bear bonz" word processor that does little except make quick jottings onto an electronic device. Now, it will become my new hand held word processor.

Notes will need a lot of help to make what is written to it a bonafide document. Here is where my desktop Commodore and GeoWrite come into play. After much experimenting, I can take documents written to Notes and upload them to my email, copy and paste the document to my Apache Open Office word processor, save to 3 1/2" disk, convert to Commodore using Big Blue Reader, and finally loaded as a file into GeoWrite. Here, in the quiet of the computer room, usually late at night, I make changes and block the document to get it ready for the return trip to the laptop.

"Wait a minute, Pops," you might be thinking, "why go through the hassle of sending it to the Commodore? You could do all that with the PC." Very true, but I personally think that an article about or including the Commodore should actually have something done to it on the actual machine. Besides, to quote Dr. Peter Venkman in the Xbox 360 game, Ghostbusters, "What's the fun in that?" Commodore is the name of the game so let's play.

Another reason why I think it's best to boomerang through the Commodore when it is to have a back up to my back up that is on a different media. I cannot count the times that I have lost data on my PC, my flash drive, and yes, even the Commodore floppy disk. I can think right now of a two part play I wrote called Mission: Messiah and Mission: Easter. I wrote this on a Commodore 128 using GeoWrite as the word processor. I then transferred these documents to my Commodore emulator using 1581Copy. There the documents sat, one complete and one near completion on my Vista OS PC until that fateful day when Hennessy, the Commodore Cat, knocked the PC onto the floor and shattering the motherboard. I shipped the laptop to Keytesville, Missouri where my friend and technician, The Vector, lived to try and extract as much of the data as possible. He succeeded in extracting Mission: Messiah, but Mission: Easter, the funniest of the two plays, lost half of its text. The Vector mailed me those files on a flash drive and I examined them. It was not good. Mr. Parker of Commodore Free was nice enough to take the files (via Internet upload) and put them back onto a Commodore 1581 floppy then shipped them overseas to me. Upon arrival I booted the disk with GeoWrite but my fears were confirmed--Mission: Easter was fifty percent gone. And my copies of the text on 5.25" disk? They also lost integrity over the years of sitting. Mr. Parker did more research on his end was able to call off the 1581 emulated image disk more of the text to Mission: Easter and sent it to me over the Internet in .txt format. I was trying to be thankful that I still had half the document but to try to call all that detail out of my memory to fix the play was going to take a lot of time. With this disaster I resolved to have back up of back ups when it comes to documents; one copy on my PC hard drive, one on my flash drive, one on Commodore 5.25" disk, and one on Commodore 3.5" disk. In the Commodore versions I have two copies per disk; one in GeoWrite and one in PET ASCII created by Wrong Is Write. I pray this fluke of computer errors can be avoided again.

It is getting harder and harder for one like myself to continue to turn to the Commodore when there are capable programs running on both PC and Mac. Sure, I sometimes take shortcuts by completely ignoring my Commodore altogether and work with only the PC, but I try only to do that when I am pressured by deadlines that I may not meet by going through the Commodore. During the times before I found Notes I was running late to even blowing off deadlines. Most editors (like Reset's) understand life gets in the way sometimes, but in my case life is constantly in the way, so much so that even time on a PC was becoming a problem let alone the Commodore. Now I don't have to work till midnight, write for two hours, sleep for two hours, and try to start a new day; I can write virtually anywhere.

Even with the applications and programs I've mentioned in this piece I wish to never persuade a user to abandon a machine like the Commodore in favor of them. I'm only describing a method that works for me and my busy lifestyle. Please, gentle reader, always go back to the source and work on your Commodore whenever you can. I long for days when I can just sit at the Commodore desk in my office, insert a 5,25" disk favorite, and just work directly with the machine. Commodores were designed in an era when things were built to last. Today's computers don't make it too far in the time trap like Commodore has.

Commodore is over thirty years old. I raise up my glass to another thirty years for it to come.

TITLE: It Might Bear Repeating

POINT OF ORIGIN: The Interface newsletter

MODE: Commentary

SYNOPSIS: Lenard apologizes for missing the 2016 CommVEx and mentions some things that he will work on and hopefully have a bigger venue for the 2017 showing.

Shift-Clr/Home

It Might Bear Repeating

It is with deep sadness that I announce here in the pages of "The Interface" that I will not be attending the 2016 CommVEx being held in Las Vegas, Nevada on the last weekend of July. At one of my four jobs, the manager wants to go see his family in Italy and his time there coincides with CommVEx. Since I went to the convention in 2015, I decided that I would go ahead and skip a year and let him see his family. I can only pray that there is a CommVEx 2017 and begin to make preparations in Kansas City for that exhibition. This is too bad for me since I was looking forward to the larger room and the chance to use the overhead projector to give everyone attending a chance to see what is going on with Commodore in the Midwest.

There's a few promises I made at CommVEx 2015 that I need to fulfill and I have yet to even begin to work on them. One is to try and fix my faulty "boot within a boot" subroutine that I discussed with readers in a previous issue or two. This problem seems to be eluding me, so I may have to subscribe that, with each four or five accesses to the main programs on the disk, that the user simply turns off, then turns back on, the Commodore. What I think may be needed is a memory "dump" of the previous program to make room for the incoming program. Right now as the program stands, each program, including the boot screens, overwrites the program presently in memory. As any novice programmer knows, this is a good way to "confuse" the Commodore, especially if the overwrite isn't complete, and garbage piles up, thus, the computer crashes.

I'm also working on revamps to a couple of programs to add extra features and make the programs overall, more user friendly. Mostly everything written on a Commodore is already user friendly because the Commodore itself is user friendly. The machine always lets you know when something initially isn't going to work right, but there are times, especially when coding in

163

BASIC, that things are coded right but phrased wrong, so the Commodore hiccups and presents something silly on the screen. This has happened to me more times than I can remember during my adventures behind the keyboard. Those moments are frustrating; those moments make you want to pull what's left of your hair out; but when the problem line is found and fixed it's like a fresh breeze wafting over you on a cool spring day as the coded text finally does what you designed it to do.

Then, as a topper to the cake, there is the ever elusive user's guide for each program that needs to be written, and, like the user's guide to "The Envelope Adddressor v4.2" (TEA v4.2), I would like to make the guides available on disk to be read on screen. I'm pretty good at writing things like articles, skits, stories, plays, etc., etc., but when it comes to writing a guide on how to do something, particularly something I coded, I stink. The user's guide to TEA 4.2 went through ten revisions on paper before I got it to where it read well and was useful to people.

I also want to take a crack at using a game construction set on the Commodore 64. I know that those people who created such software really tried to make game building easy, but there are still hose heads like me who need additional tutoring to make sure I understand everything correctly. I've been advised by FCUG that all such construction sets are available on the Internet in some sort of image format, but it would cost more money for me to buy the proper software, hardware, and cables than to just check eBay and bid on the proper item needed. Sure, I take a chance that I will spend good money on bad product but with the lack of proper Internet hookups for the Commodore, this, as stated before, is more cost effective.

Finally, as I promised at the CommVEx 2015, and posted on YouTube, I hope to have done a first draft of a new Commodore book. The good news is that I have several essays and articles to choose from; the bad news is that I have several essays and articles to choose from. In "Run/Stop-Restore: 10th Anniversary Edition" I had limited collection, which made selection easy, but now, six years and three magazines to write for, this may be harder than I thought. I only want to choose the best of the best for the new book and that's a chore in itself. Also, don't forget that I'm also working on my skits and plays for churches. As of this writing, I am one year behind on promised release of my new skit book, and I'm falling behind every day. I have to apologize for this. I see these mega-ministers releasing at least one book a year and thought I could do the same. It was later realized that these people have a warehouse full of staff that can take his notes and write up beautiful prose wherein I work with only my closest friends who volunteer their time and talent to make me look good. They do a dynamite job and I wouldn't switch them for a paid professional at all, but I have to meet them half way and write the manuscripts. For those of you who follow my writing career outside FCUG and Commodore, Volume Three of my puppet skit series is going through a second re-write as, when I looked at the book as a whole, I was not satisfied with my results, so I decided to go through the entire manuscript and start making changes in writing, style, format, and descriptions. I hope to get back onto this project soon.

I also wanted to, as a consolation for not being able to attend CommVEx, make a video of myself presenting the same programs I did at CommVEx 2015, but with a lot more detail than what I presented at the meeting. I wanted to have the venue at the church I attend, but, because of the rise of lawsuits against churches coming from the LGBT community, my church has suspended all extra curricular activities that are not church related. Even though I am a member of the church, the Commodore machine is not, so I cannot make the video in a large venue. I can make it here at the Roach Center For BASIC Commodore Studies but it would take some positioning to get the best camera in such a small room like where my Commodore 128 resides, and there is no room anywhere else in the RC4BCS to get a good video of the layout. Back when I was making programs left and right for the Commodore 64, and before the invention of the Digital Video Disc, I would plug my Commodore's video cable into the back of a Video Cassette Recorder and record what was being broadcasted from the machine onto video tape, then show the tape at the Kansas City Commodore meeting along with my standing there giving a play by play description of what was being shown on screen. We pretty much do that now with the meetings, but we usually have a central Commodore computer to work from that is already hooked up to a video display.

I'm sorry if I am beginning to sound like a skipping CD and repeating myself in these pages, but it doesn't hurt to go over again what I have said before in earlier issues and bundle it up, once again, into a single piece. I have so many things planned for my Commodore work that I would like to take a year off from working and just get it all done in that time span. But I know me, and the me I know would not sit right down and work on all these projects but find excuses not to work on them. This is the fault of the lack of discipline I encountered in my younger days which is carrying over into present times. If given the chance to do it over again, I would definitely work harder on being more consistent and less flighty, then I would have the self control to get things done in a timely manner. But be that as it may, one must allow the picking up of all the broken pieces of your life and allow them to be assembled into a functioning fashion.

TITLE: Once And Future Commodore

POINT OF ORIGIN: The Interface newsletter

MODE: Commentary

SYNOPSIS: Lenard gives his perspective on the 2015 CommVEx Commodore show and how he plans to attend the 2016 show and what he plans on taking to it

Shift-Clr/Home

Once And Future Commodore

CommVEx, CommVEx, CommVEx, what can one say about CommVEx that has not already been said? FresnoDick's report both on his website and in "The Interface" is well accepted. My co-conspirator who works with me at church on Sunday mornings has written his view on the show, which was NOT cleared by me or any of the officers of FCUG, so he's on my "naughty" list for Christmas this year for not checking in, but, then again, we are suppose to be a country of "free speech" so he shouldn't have to report to me to express his canine opinions to the press.

So what can *I* say about CommVEx that has not already been said? Only that this year's CommVEx was the best collection of Commodore minds and fun seekers that I have ever attended. It was great to meet and actually speak with the son of the late Jack Tramiel, Leonard, and Commodore 128 creator and designer, Bil Herd. That crazy dog I brought with me from Kansas City actually got to interview Mr. Herd, and he posted his interview on YouTube for all to see. I know I shouldn't plug Theo's video in my article after what he has done but when you catch someone as big in Commodore as Bil Herd being playful with such an animal like Theo, you gotta broadcast it. So, type in the YouTube search engine THEO IN VEGAS (all caps) and look for the puppet sheepdog, it would be worth your watching.

Like I said, the 2015 CommVEx was probably the creme del la creme of all the CommVEx shows I've attended and read about. We had big celebrities and fun, fun, fun all around. But, alas, not all was perfect at the show and that was mainly due to me.

Ladies and gentlemen, my apologies to you for such a poor showing of what we in the Midwest are doing with Commodore at the show. I had twelve months to get ready and make a large presentation, and that was my plan from August 2014 to July 2015, but, do you know that familiar voice that lurks in your mind called Procrastination that always tells you to do what needs to be done later, or next week, or next month? Then, when the newly allotted time arrives, there are more pressing issues that arises so I, again, push the time back. What little was seen at CommVEx by me was assembled and finalized in a three week period between July 4th and show time. And then, at presentation time, I only show one of many programs present on my "5 Program Bonus Disk" and cut off any question and answer time since I knew I would not be able to answer efficiently inquiries from such a studious group. I also did not plug well my Commodore book so people had no idea how to respond when I asked for a show of support for a sequel to the same. An uninformed group does not know how to vote on a proposal. Even my back woods jokes I lamely tried to tell backfired as I poorly delivered the material. All in all, a pretty lousy presentation on the part of The Fat Man.

Now the question that is to be asked here is: What am I going to do to fix the problem? Well, I need to join my local chapter of "Procrastinator's Anonymous," but they keep postponing their meetings till the next month. What about getting off my lazy, fat, flatulent fanny and get things done? Hmm. Sounds like a good plan but it may lack execution. This whole thing measures around a simple deal of time management. It is true, dear reader, that ye olde Fat Guy here does put in a lots of hours doing three jobs and working overtime so, thinking on those lines, maybe it's not a matter of procrastination, but of a lack of free time to work on all things Commodore. Not everyone can be a Robert Bernardo and focus all our energies on this fantastic single board wonder (just kidding!), but, at the same instance, I think I must review the past twenty four hours and discover where my "free" time, if truly any, has gone.

After a thorough investigation of a random twenty four period it has come to my conclusion that a lot of my free time (where I'm doing little to nothing) is actually embedded within my work times, like breaks, lunches, and layovers. I've ran into this problem before when I was editor of the Commodore Users Group of Kansas City's newsletter, "Ryte Bytes" and, writing wise, the answer came in the form of a little program embedded within the iPhone 4 simply called Notes. Notes is just what it claims to be, a note taking program for the quick jotting down of information. I have used Notes in the past to make writing deadlines by typing in the words I want to say and forwarding those notes to my personal email, then copying the document out of email and pasting it into my computer's word processor, where final blocking and editing are done. The iPhone 4 has long since been disconnected from the network so I have to wait until I get to a WiFi hot spot to send the document through the email.

With that problem solved for the most part, what about programming in Commodore BASIC? How will that be accomplished? I've been thinking about that and -- I'm drawing a blank. Unless some of our Commodore geniuses out in cyberspace can come up with an application for either Apple or Android, we may be at an impasse, albeit a temporary one. My oldest son, RJ, has been looking off and on for an app to allow him to play his favorite Commodore games that he grew up with, like "Hardball!" The app I would be looking at would be more of a "swap" program between Commodore computers and the device. Most likely a third party computer running either a Windows or Mac OS would be necessary to make such a product work properly. But, as always, the final denominator comes down to money, money, money! How much can be made on such an application? If you're asking this Redneck then my answer is simple: I don't know. Like pretty much everything else it would all come down to how well the product is marketed. I'm having my own personal battles with marketing on all the books I have in circulation. I'm not the one to ask on this.

Well, with all that ironed out it looks like this old man has a plan as to what needs to be done in order to make his Commodore time more productive both on as well as away from the keyboard. I'm confident that a better showing on Commodore from the Midwest will be able to grace next year's CommVEx. It looks like a good time all around the Roach Center For BASIC Commodore Studies as we prepare for same...

TITLE: In Search Of Specific Software

POINT OF ORIGIN: The Interface newsletter

MODE: Commentary

SYNOPSIS: Lenard tells of his journey to look for Bible based software games for the Commodore 64/128 and finds only one source on the entire Internet. Read what it is in this piece.

Shift-Clr/Home

In Search Of Specific Software

You come up to the spired building, curious to learn what on the other side of the doors, which itself has the shape of a small wooden cross affixed to it. The doors open effortlessly, allowing you to enter into the welcoming foyer. Not too far into the structure you see a booted Commodore 64, which stands like a lone sentinel in this, somehow hallowed building. As you walk up to the computer you see on the screen a loaded program. The program seems to invite to grab the standing joystick off a little to the right and start game play. You pick up the joystick, glare at the game on the computer screen, and let the fun begin...

Nice set up. The Commodore computer set up all nice and neat in the sanctuary of a church asking attendees to stop by and give him a shot at the game loaded into memory. Of course, it all depends on what up on the screen. I sat down in my computer room and started searching Google to find Christian software especially coded for the Commodore computer, narrowing my search down to either the Commodore 64 or the Commodore 128.

One thing I instantly found out was there were a significant amount of Bible reading and study programs, but as I searched further I found out that these pieces of software were quickly abandoned for the larger memory and faster processors offered by both IBM and Apple computers. The good news is that before software developers moved off the Commodore platform they did write and distribute these studies for the Commodore and they are still available for the machine from third and fourth party dealers as well as private collectors. Finding a good, solid, original copy of the programs may be hard to locate in this, the 21st century. If if wasn't for the preservation efforts of those few who can transpose Commodore computer programs to the Internet there would be nothing left of them. The best location I've found for Bible software I found is: www.biblecom.tripod.com. The site is monitored by a pastor of a fellowship in Lima, New York. I do not know how old this information on the Internet is so I will state that I am not responsible for the accuracy of this information.

This little bit of data is great for older children and adults who use the Commodore for study and productivity but what about those younger than, say, fourteen? Is there anything in the Commodore universe for them? Fear not, true believer, there is!

There is listed on Amazon copies of the book, "Bible Computer Games Book 2" made for the Commodore 64 and other formats that use BASIC as the programming template. This book comes out right after the release of Volume One of the same work but for different formats older than the Commodore. Authored by Mr. Conrod, this book teaches both the Bible in type in games as well as showing the reader Commodore BASIC. It's hard to get full data on this book from Amazon, but they give enough information to let the shopper know what kind of games there are. I will have to buy the book (it's out of print but Amazon has used copies on sale for about $3.68) and see for myself what the book contains and give all the readers of "The Interface" a full report.

When I brought this idea of writing an article about Christian software for the Commodore up to Robert Bernardo and FresnoDick, they suggested that I put a blurb out on Homestead and see what bites I get. I remember the days of discussing such subjects like this during my BBS cruising days and if you mention the name of Jesus in any other form than a swear word then you start a firestorm. I don't know if I'm up to the defense of the gospel online. I sucked as an apologist then and I suck as an apologist now -- and all I'm looking for is Commodore software in relation to the Bible. I debated with atheists, Hindus, Catholics, the KKK; everyone, and all I wanted to do is what I aforementioned. I know that 1 Peter warns me to be ready to give an account of the faith that lives in me but COME ON! I just want to chat on the boards or play an online game. We're suppose to be in an Age of Enlightenment, but it's only for the philosophical set and not the crazies. Oh well, I'll take a stab at Homestead for that data but I must admit I'm a little leery. When I made an investigative search on pornography for the Commodore I was directed to one website that has it all so there was no need to search further, and some of the sights on this website would make a hardened Marine blush!

I know that I have got into debates with a few "super geeks" that claimed that the computer is completely man made and there was no "god" involved. This would follow the premise of man trying to make himself out to be THE God, and, well, I was told that if one person will not listen to reason, you move on to the next person. I know that in the movies, like "Star Trek: The Motion Picture," people believe that computers can amass so much knowledge that the machine will achieve a consciousness. I'm not too sure. We have a lot of machines already here in the 21st century that have a lot of data and they still act like computers, requiring a designer and a programmer to make them into what they are. I'm amazed as to how far graphics and memory have come since the days of the Commodore and people are still expanding on such devices to make them more powerful and faster, but I don't think that anyone can beat the good ol' calculating machine that was put into the head of every human being on the planet. It's still faster, more productive, and has not needed an upgrade for the past who-knows-how many years. The reason why I was told there was not any Christian games for the Commodore back in the day was it did not fit the "genre" of the computer. What does that mean? I thought "programming" was just that and it did not matter what market you were trying to reach as long as said market was willing to shell out greenbacks to get the product offered by the market, be it Christian, porn, or whatever. The last I looked money was money no matter if it was being handed to you by a priest or a pimp. Something must have got lost in translation. So, here is where we sit on the subject with very little data to go on even from such a large search engine as Google. Sure, the market corrected itself as computers got faster and held more data, but for the Commodore, it just isn't much.

TITLE: Programming Conundrums

POINT OF ORIGIN: The Interface newsletter

MODE: Commentary

SYNOPSIS: Lenard is now thankful for his poor showing at CommVEx 2015 because the software he intended to sell at the show has some bugs he was unaware of. Read how Lenard found the bugs and his intended plan to attack them in this genre specific piece.

Shift-Clr/Home

Programming Conundrums

Ladies and gentlemen of the Fresno Commodore User Group, I am befuddled and bewildered. I've sat down with the five programs that I presented to the Commodore public at the 2015 CommVEx and I really don't know what to do with them. Just like jello, there's always room for more, but I don't know what that "more" is, at least not by this writing. What I think I need to do is stand back and make an overall assessment of the programs both as a whole and as individual Commodore works. Putting the entire works into a single package was a great idea, but, and I'm sure I've stated this before, each program keeps crashing into each other as a battle for the buffer ensues.

For example, I was paying my first of the month bills one evening using "The Ledger," my debt tracking program for the Commodore 64. As I started prodding along and typing into the Commodore 64 all the data of who gets paid where with what money, everything was fine. Then as I was working on some hospital bills the Commodore came up with an "OUT OF MEMORY" error message. This never happened when "The Ledger" was a stand alone program separated onto its own disk but now that its part of a conglomerate of programs it starts acting up. To get out of the error message I typed RUN after the blinking cursor and "The Ledger" ran fine to finish the rest of the bills I was cataloging.

The one thing "The Ledger" does that none of the other five programs in the package do is perform a validation sweep of the entire disk that the program resides on. I felt it was important to have one of the five programs do the validation sweep because programs like "The Ledger" and "Money Manager 2K" do a lot of data transfers from Commodore to disk and back. Once a user gets used to finding his or her way around "The Ledger" they can start swapping information quick enough with just a few key strokes that the disk drive doesn't have time to settle down after a spin on the hub before data is being swapped again. This could have caused the OUT OF MEMORY error message I experienced on that day I was paying bills. Also, I know from experience that daisy chaining programs together is a hectic way to form a disk conglomerate. It is better for the function of the programs to be merged into one single massive program that requires no loading and dumping to the disk drive. However, I still have yet to find that certain Commodore program, either commercially made or freeware, which will do that particular job. The problem with making several individual programs into one major program is memory capacity. Remember, we are only dealing with 64K of space on the standard Commodore computer, but for simple ease and flow of data, merging is best. I know merging programs for the Commodore exist; I just have to find them.

Daisy chaining usually causes one program to overwrite another. If any data from the standing program remains during the overwrite, the Commodore figures the remaining data is part of the new matrix coming in and tries to run both together, thus creating an error message requiring a total shutdown and reboot of the machine and the loss of any unsaved data. The loss of data is something I try to avoid when I sit down at my Commodore machine to code a program, thus I always have several points in a Lenard Roach program where data is dumped onto disk before any further work can be done. It's something my Commodore teacher, Carl Zuel, taught me: "Save early and save often." This little philosophy has saved my programming bacon several times during my journeys through the maze of coding; but daisy chaining, well, that's an animal of complete mystery where confusion reigns supreme. When it came to daisy chaining all five of the programs on the "5 Program Bonus Disk" I demonstrated at the 2015 CommVEx, everything worked well at home, but boy, at the show ... It was, shall we say, a pain to deal with.

I've been doing some research with a few manuals that I have here at the Roach Center For BASIC Commodore Studies and I've been reading about what the CLR command will do. Supposedly, CLR will remove all data, variables, and pointers off the machine and set everything to zero without disturbing actual program content but it must be used before any numerical data is entered. My programs usually carry very little numerical data except for "The Ledger" which is based on numbers when it comes to calculating the information in paying bills and how much is left to pay (basic addition and subtraction). Really, it can't hurt much to try CLR in a program or two and see if that will eliminate the overlap problems. I was also looking into the NEW command, but that would eliminate the program in memory as well as any data; not a good idea, but at least does what I am looking for, just, well, it's overkill. Therefore I'm looking for something between CLR and NEW, where CLR takes care of a little and NEW takes care of it all and then some. Man, the life of a Commodore BASIC programmer -- sheesh!

And, I'm sure this makes the problem worse, the "Main Boot Screen" where a user selects which program to boot, is itself a stand alone program. So, in essence, I'm trying to daisy chain six programs together into one large conglomerate of software, trying my best to make the "5 Program Bonus Disk" function like a commercial piece of software that a person would find at the computer store. Maybe I should realize that I'm a small little minnow in the pond of big Commodore catfish and that my existence in the pond is based on pure blessings from above that I haven't been eaten by any of the larger fish yet. I know that my efforts don't go wasted in vain, but still it would be great to have this Commodore plan come together. What I really should have done was allow copies of the existing programs go out to those who would like to work with it and see if they can offer suggestions on how to make all those programs cooperate together.

When I was working on "Check It Out," I took myself and the program to Wichita State University to see Carl, who was working on his degree in business back then. Carl, at the time, was one of the head geeks on campus and almost everyone at the university would come to him for computer help and advice. I showed Carl (on his Commodore 128) what it was that I was doing and what I would like for "Check It Out" to do. The first thing he noticed right off was my lack of checksums in the program. "You need more error messages," he said. I told him that only adults would be working with "Check It Out" and therefore checksums were not necessary. Carl gave me the funniest look and proceeded to give me a lecture on Beginning BASIC Programming. "Home computing is basically a new field," he would say. "If you don't want your program to crash on the user every two or three punches of the keyboard, you have to include checksums. Tell the user what he can and cannot do." He proceeded then to add a few short subroutines that would help me build into a larger base of "do's and don'ts" for the average user. I took Carl's help and advice (with a little grain of salt (hey, he is my Commodore teacher after all!)) and went back to Kansas City to finish the rest of the program to get ready for the, then, last issue of RUN magazine.

I told you that story to tell you this: I didn't add even half of the checksums I did in "Check It Out" in "The Ledger," "Checkmate," or "TEA v4.2" for the simple reason that most users of the Commodore now are anywhere from thirty years old and older and, with the technology advances that have been made in the computer and electronics fields since the hey days of Commodore, more than likely a complete file of checksums and error messages are not necessary. I've added a few in my programs like file name lengths not past sixteen characters and simple "FILE NOT FOUND" messages. Usually, I set the BASIC commands to loop back to the beginning of the program if the user tries to do anything to program was not written to do. I find such coding, though I'm sure necessary (Carl would not steer me wrong), it was tedious, especially if the program was in great length and many checksums were needed.

With all the befuddlement and bewilderment that I've been experiencing when it comes to working with the programs, I'm having troubles trudging on in this journey of coding. I think I might be the only one in Kansas City, Kansas who still works with a Commodore machine on a regular basis. Most users now go with emulators instead of making space for the real machine so getting help locally seems to be limited. I know that those of the Fresno Commodore User Group are always willing to help, so I may just start knocking on some doors and seeing what can be done.

Shift-Clr/Home

TITLE: The Time Is At Hand

POINT OF ORIGIN: The Interface newsletter

MODE: Commentary

SYNOPSIS: Lenard confesses his sin of procrastination and gives a list of what he plans to show at CommVEx 2015, ready or not.

Shift-Clr/Home

The Time Is At Hand

In one month, Lenard should be able to attend the 2015 CommVEx held in Las Vegas, Nevada.

One month?

YARGH!

(Thud.)

Huh? What? Oh, sorry. I must have passed out for a moment, but the shock that, after all this time of waiting, CommVEx is less than a month away from being a reality. How are you set for this once a year event? I must admit …

… I AIN'T GOT SQUAT ONE THING DONE!

I had this big list of stuff to do in the year that I had to prepare for the show, and I didn't even so much as sit down at the Commodore in the computer room and get things done. I wanted to program some games using the game construction sets I have here at the Roach Center, but I never sat down to learn the programs functions. Sometimes I think I'm too old to learn anything new, even when it comes to the Commodore, but that could also be called one simple word … LAZINESS!

Yup, I never had the desire to sit down and go through the programs and see what needs to be done. I'm more interested in writing my own code from a blank screen instead of using code provided by someone else, even if that code is to help me write code. Pride? Ego? Stupidity? Number three is my option, but number two is looking kind of right, too. Maybe its all three. I don't know for sure, but one thing I am sure of is that I had one year to get all this straighten out and I didn't.

So, Fat Man, what are you going to do for a presentation when to get to CommVEx?

Well, let me say that this year wasn't a total loss, just a mostly total loss. I did sit down over the winter and come up with my new "5 Program Bonus Disk" which contains five of the programs I use the most on the Commodore, a couple of which I wrote myself. Like I said in past issues of "The Interface," this is still a project in the works, but I will be offering it as a developer's disk for anyone who would want to try and make more out of it than I have. I know that when I demonstrate this package to the CommVEx attendees, there will be some suggestions come up for items that can be added to the disk to make it more user friendly and more helpful for those who access the programs. These five programs are:

"TEA v4.2" – The envelope writing program that addresses envelopes using a standard Commodore printer and your own envelopes. Most people nowadays use the Internet to pay bills and avoid spending the extra forty seven cents it takes to mail a letter anymore. I know that as a PC user as well as a Commodore user, this feature of modern computers is handy and makes for quick posting of a debt owed while good old fashioned snail mail takes the usual three to five days to get an envelope from one point to another. In many cases using an on line payment system costs the user more than a stamp and therefore not worth it. If you have such a website that forces you to pay like some of mine, then "TEA v4.2" is a good program for you. As for a printer, those who still have the good old fashioned 9 pin printer around, it would be good to pull it out of storage, blow off the dust, and bring it back into service.

"Check It Out" – Even though this program is now the property of RUN magazine, and whoever now has the rights to RUN's programs, this update to the original magazine edition rearranges the line definitions and gives the program access to it's sister program "Check Mate" which will be discussed further down the page. "Check It Out" is the check printing program that, with a standard 9 pin printer, you can print on the face of any wallet size check the needed information and print that data onto the check. The November/December 1992 issue of RUN has the best description of how the program works. Please check it out (no pun intended).

"Check Mate" – When making out a check for the same amount over and over each month, "Check It Out" can take up some time as you re-input the data each month. "Check Mate" allows "Check It Out" sequential data to be saved in a simple one block file that is now accessible with the new version of "Check It Out" offered on the 5 Program Bonus Disk. "Check It Out" will ask for "Check Mate" data files each pass of the program and a simple Y or N answer will send the user to the appropriate subroutine.

"The Ledger" – This is my latest program work that came to my warped mind. Most people already have a ledger keeping program in their Commodore collection. I am hoping that this BASIC, simple written program will be easier to use and with the code not compressed into a encryption file, it can be modified by each individual user to meet special specifications. There is much work that can probably be added to this program, and when I get to CommVEx I will be coming with notebook in hand to write down any suggestions that come from our austere audience. In short, "The Ledger" keeps track of who's paid and when then saves that data as well as any payments made in a short one block sequential file. This file can be manipulated from any of the menu driven commands written in the program code and saved into either a new file or the same file depending on the preference of the user.

"Money Manager with EZ Budget" – This is a program I spent a great deal of time typing in from a RUN magazine and is being offered on the 5 Program Bonus Disk as a helpful tool to keep an electronic checkbook and budgeting form on your Commodore. Even in the 21st century where check writing is almost obsolete this program can still be used to do balancing and budgeting information. I do not own the rights to this program but since it is freeware offered in RUN magazine I think a free distribution of the work is okay.

All these programs are daisy chained together with a master boot program that allows a user to choose which program to access, and also, when done, the program accessed will sweep back and reboot the master boot program in case there are other programs on the 5 Program Bonus Disk the user wishes to use.

WHAT I NEEDED/WANTED TO DO: It seems that the master boot program gets bogged down in the buffer of the Commodore when too many of the programs on the disk are entered. I've been studying the online versions of the Commodore Users Guide and what might fix the problem is adding a CLR command at the tail of each program before looping back to the master boot program. Also, combining the programs into one massive program may also fix it, but I will need a merging file to make all of that work. With CommVEx so close by, I will have to work on this after the show.

In "The Ledger" there are more things that can probably be put in, like setting a date in the program and having each sequential file check the date and see how long (in days) it is before the bill becomes overdue. Also a warning screen stating that a bill is past due might be a possibility. I'm just a simple redneck programmer and sometimes I'll get an idea but lack the algebra and proper Commodore expressions to make it work. Again, more study and a visit to the Commodore forums online might prove to have the information needed to make ideas work.

Most programmers in Commodore have moved on from simple BASIC into more complex programming languages but I still find a bit of comfort when reading a program text and deciphering what it means and how it relates to the text as a whole.

ALSO COMING TO COMMVEX – I will be bringing more copies of my book, "Run/Stop-Restore: 10th Anniversary Edition" to be won and sold at the show and I will take some time to plug it in front of our audience. I'm currently in negotiations with my printing company to try and get a deal from them especially for CommVEx attendees. Visiting authorhouse.com has shown my book has come down in price a little so maybe I can forward the savings onto attendees.

I will also be bringing and demonstrating the "Obligator Coordinator V2.0" which is the father to "The Ledger." This program does what "The Ledger" does but with a little more pomp and a lot of glitches. Hopefully we all will be able to see together why this project was scrapped and maybe, with a little TLC from CommVEx attendees, we can make a Commodore program phoenix rise from the ashes.

To entertain the kids back home, I will be bringing Theodore Sheepdog, the church puppet, to interview those who wish to be put on YouTube displaying their wares. Theodore will also be about Las Vegas having fun and hopefully finding some kid friendly characters to interview on the Fremont Street Experience that won't cost an arm and a leg in fees. A reminder to those who wish to cooperate: At the church is a fully functional C128 complete with monitor and drives that the kids in Kansas City has access to. Maybe a little demonstration of what you do for them will be helpful for them to use the machine.

Shift-Clr/Home

TITLE: And The Beat Goes On

POINT OF ORIGIN: The Interface newsletter

MODE: Commentary

SYNOPSIS: Lenard tells the reader how he was taught to build a good working, stand alone boot program/subroutine that works well with any BASIC program. He also congratulates The Fresno Commodore User Group for 33 years of existence.

Shift-Clr/Home

And The Beat Goes On

When you sit down and look at some of the things you've haven't worked on over the past several months, you begin to see places where an improvement could be made. I've made some adjustments to all my programs except "TEA v4.2" which appears to be the only program that seems to be all right just the way it is. I did create a boot screen for it that will allow the user to run the program without having to actually type "RUN" and press RETURN.

There is a little string of POKE commands that helped me create the boot command, but first the programmer needs to find the quotient for "X". To do this, the programmer loads the program he wants to make a boot for, then, without running the program, type on an empty line the following command:

PRINTPEEK(46)

A number will appear below the command line. The programmer will take this total given by the PEEK command and add 1. For the sake of argument let's say that PRINTPEEK(46) equals 75; add 1 to this number (76). SYS out the program using the line SYS64738 or just reboot the Commodore, whichever is easier, then load the boot program. You can either LIST the program code lines or just make your command line number 1. Type the following BASIC line (still using 76 as our sample number):

1 POKE46,76:POKE48,76:POKE50,76:POKE52,76

.. and press RETURN. Resave the boot program using Commodore's "@0:" command for replace and save. To test to see if your boot program works make sure you have a LOAD"[program name]",DN (device number) somewhere within your boot program that the program can reference to boot the main program. I usually put the [program name] and DN at the end of my boot program so there will be no confusion to the Commodore reading the program. Load your boot program and see if your boot loads your main program. If not, then recheck your PEEKS, POKES, and your LOAD commands.

The reason for the POKE commands is to make sure the Commodore loads the entire program. Booting a program from a stand alone subroutine usually causes either the boot program or the main program to fail to load completely, thus causing an "ERROR IN LINE X" message when ran. I'm hoping to make a master boot program that will boot the separate boot programs, that will in turn boot the main program. I have a type in program from "Run" magazine that creates a LOAD and RUN command so all a user has to is type LOAD"[boot program]",8,1 and the program will boot without having to type in the RUN command.

The Master Boot program I've written using the "Screen Gem" low res graphics program by Mr. Godfrey allows a user to load any of the 5 programs I've either written or updated on my own. By selecting numbers 1 through 5 the user can boot either "Check It Out," "Checkmate," "The Ledger," "TEA v4.2," or "Money Manager 2K." Adjustments have been made to some of the programs so all the data from each program can be saved to the master disk and accessed without causing any crossing of data between programs. "TEA v4.2" uses either a "T/" or an "F/" prefix on each data file name, and now "The Ledger" uses the British Pound sign as a prefix for it's data files. This way a user can have the same data file name for each program thus saving the problem of memorizing all those different data file names. Only "Checkmate" uses the standard data file format while "Money Manager 2K" only uses two data file names; one called "Budget" and the other is the number of the month and year of the electronic check book.

Hopefully, I have not caused any confusion to those reading the above comments, but if I get to go to the 2015 CommVEx, I will be able to show during a demonstration exactly how this programming idea works.

I was looking online at one of the hotel finding websites and found no rooms available near the Plaza Hotel where the convention is being held; even the Plaza Hotel is booked during that weekend for the show. The Roach Center team may have to stay off Fremont Street and drive in to the convention and hopefully find parking. I was told to try Expedia.com and see if there are hotels on that website.

I'm still trying to decide if I should bring with me some books other than "Run/Stop-Restore: 10th Anniversary Edition," just to show what I have been working on over the years. I'm finding out that those writers who publish books every few months have a team of editors and stenographers working for them so they can get this done. My team is staffed at three with myself being the main writer, editor, and book format expert. I shouldn't be so hard on myself when I can't get a book out at least once a year; also, I have to work regular jobs to maintain my lifestyle and the lifestyles of those who stay with me.

I have yet to learn how to use some of the software for game creation and, in fact, I'm a little hesitant in working with them. Until I learn the ins and outs of gaming (which I am trying to learn on my own time from watching games being played on today's consoles) I may have to live with just the confines of Commodore gaming and forget the knowledge I got from gaming. Today's games are more interactive stories than they are games and I don't know if I can come up with something that will be of interest for Commodore users. However, I will never know unless I sit down and try. Finding minutes between jobs is becoming a new challenge for me, but there is time if I (like I've said a million times before) just take a minute and work on what I want to.

The collection of Commodore equipment I got over Christmas is slowly finding homes but those who have received the machines are looking for software and turning to me to provide it. So far all the software I got with the collection will not boot on the collective Commodores but any software I've written or got from FCUG will boot fine. I do not know the difference between the disks for both the CUGKC collection and mine were stored in environmentally controlled areas. I've even had a 1571 disk drive go down due to this malicious software. I am looking for someone who knows how to align the precarious 1571 with its dual heads. My former Commodore repairman here in Kansas City has suggested that the software from the CUGKC may just be dirty from just sitting and, in turn, transferring the dirt to the heads of all my machines. I'll have to check for dirt when it comes to booting the given software.

FCUG's famous FresnoDick and informed me via email that, if I get to go to CommVEx, he will have waiting for me a decently working Commodore SX64. The SX64 is my favorite Commodore computer to use because of it's portability and the two I have presently in my collection are non functional; one because of a faulty disk drive and the other (acquired from the CUGKC collection) is in need of keyboard repair and other serious maintenance. If it's okay with Robert Bernardo, I may pawn these two machines off onto him to take to Ray for repair and pick them up at the 2016 CommVEx. I don't know if either USPS or UPS will ship the big Commodore SX64 for a reasonable price from the West Coast to my home in Redneckville, USA but I can always investigate.

In closing, I would personally like to congratulate the Fresno Commodore User Group for achieving 33 years of Commodore computing. Newsletters like "The Interface" and other Commodore publications throughout the world help keep the

Commodore spirit alive and, if you're not careful, will produce something new that will be of benefit to the Commodore user and the world in general. I am thankful that I get to be a part of that genre that helps make Commodore the best in the computer world.

Shift-Clr/Home

TITLE: Christmas Comes Early To The Roach Center

POINT OF ORIGIN: The Interface newsletter

MODE: Story

SYNOPSIS: Lenard gives a play by play description of how he acquired the old Commodore Users Group of Kansas City's complete collection of computers and how he dealt with this Commodore mother load.

Shift-Clr/Home

Christmas Comes Early To The Roach Center

It was a surprise email that came into my inbox one frosty day in November. The subject line said "Commodore Stuff."

"Lenard (it began), are you still into Commodore? I have a lot of stuff that you can have. Please call me anytime. Jack." Jack left his phone number along with the post.

Jack was the treasurer of the Commodore Users Group of Kansas City from at least 1995 until the club's disbandment early in the 21st century. I served the CUGKC as its last president. I signed the papers that sent the club's treasury as a donation to the Children's Mercy Hospital in honor of my son who was a patient there in 2004. Since the club's demise, Jack has been sitting on a stock of Commodore 64s, 128s, various disk drives, and a large assortment of software all this time, using his own resources to keep them at the proper room temperatures. He was now contacting me and asking if I wanted to take possession of the entire collection. I printed the email and put it in my lunch box (aka my briefcase) and made an appointment over the phone to pick up as much as I could in one trip in my small 1997 Plymouth Neon.

One thing I have been trying to do, even as club president, was take a look at all that Jack has stored in his basement when it came to Commodore equipment. Before time I had no storage for all the equipment, and as the years wore on, Jack set several units (both working and non-working) out on the curb for the junk collectors and the trash man. Now here in 2014 I had a place for all of the machinery in my very own house, and a computer room, to put it in.

I stopped in on a Tuesday before Thanksgiving at Jack's place in Kansas City, just minutes before a person would get to Grandview. Jack's wife was waiting for me at the door. She let me down to the basement where Jack was already starting the job of sorting the Commodore hardware and software. Jack instructed me to drive the Neon down the driveway leading to the back of the house and back it up to the garage door. A short minute later I had the passenger's door open and the seat slid forward (my 97 is a two door).

I wandered like a kid in a candy story through the shelves of Commodore equipment and software wondering what I should load first. It was a quick realization that I was not going to be able to load everything into the car on one trip, so I asked Jack if it was all right that I took the hardware first, then came back before Christmas for the software. He consented.

I started with the 1581 disk drives since they are a rare find anywhere and loaded them into the trunk of the car. I can always use an extra 1581 since this is a main machine for my conversion of texts from Commodore into PC and Jack had a few. I then loaded two full tubs of cables and cords into the back seat behind the driver since the driver's seat was broken from a car crash a few months back. After that, I found the 1571 disk drives and started stacking then deep into the trunk of the car. Now came the beauty of loading the ever famous Commodore 128s. As I loaded each computer I checked for markings to see if they may have JiffyDOS installed, and most of the units did. This was a great find since my personal C128 was almost shot due to constant use and I was going to replace my existing unit with one of Jack's computers. Finally came the Commodore 64s. Most of these units had JiffyDOS, and even one was still in the box. It was hard to believe that even after loading all this equipment into the Neon I still had some room left. Now I started loading up joysticks and any loose cables that might be in the basement. Even with all this I had just enough room for two boxes of 5.25 disks to sit on top of everything, but before I buttoned up the car I put a final item into the back seat – a Commodore monitor that was still hooked up and ready for use.

The car was packed to capacity. My years as a driver has taught me to allocate my space well in the Neon. This is where putting together puzzles with Mom during my growing up years paid off, too. I gently shut both the passenger's door and the trunk lid and turned to Jack and shook his hand. I promised him I would be back for the software before the end of the Advent season, which he said would be okay but to be sure not to forget to come for it.

Time and temperature were working against me. The sun was already down and we didn't make it to 35 degrees as a high that day, and my domicile in Kansas City, Kansas was a good 45 minutes away, and it was highway rush hour. The equipment in the cabin of the car would be fine with the heaters running but it was the stuff in the trunk that I wanted to get home before things got too cold. None to worry as I found out that a quick shot down I-435 west to Metcalf Avenue/US 169 north put me on the right road home. Before long I was backing into my driveway on Corona Avenue and ready to unload my Commodore treasure into the house.

Calibur, my son, was sitting on the sofa playing a game on the Xbox when I came through the door with the first load of equipment from the trunk.

"What the **** are you going to do with all of that stuff, Dad?" he asked after looking up from a save point in his game.

I explained to him that, once everything has been tested, I was going to make one complete Commodore 128 system available for purchase at the church's Sunday School Store and another complete 128 system will go as a gag gift for the poor soul who's name I pulled out of the basket for Secret Santa at the convenience store.

"What about the C64s?" he asked.

Hmm. Good question. I got about five Commodore 64s with the collection and really don't have a use for them since the good people at Commodore were smart enough to include a C64 inside every C128 built. However, I have noticed that some cartridges and RAM expansion units will not cooperate with the C128 but only on actual C64 hardware. I'll probably sell some units on eBay and take the money to pay for more Commodore goodies. Like I said earlier, most units came with JiffyDOS and therefore should provide a good dime or two on the market.

It took me about four hours to unload the Neon and test as many different pieces of hardware that I could put in my bedroom (the computer room had no access to power with all the newly acquired Commodore equipment taking up space). When I got done I reduced the Commodore equipment down to four C128s, two 1571s, three 1581s, and five C64s. After going through the gear I did have an aftermarket 1541 drive out of the whole collection that was also working well so I may keep that for myself. I know that one of the C128s with JiffyDOS will go onto my personal Commodore stand to replace my failing machine. I also enjoy the 1571 with JiffyDOS, but my initial testing in the bedroom with the hardware showed me that a JiffyDOS 128 and a JiffyDOS 1571 do not like each other. JiffyDOS in the 128 had to be disabled to access the JiffyDOS in the 1571. I'm sure that my testing on these items was erroneous and without proper instructions on how to use JiffyDOS, I am just flying blind here.

Nothing felt better than to have some Commodore units to glean from instead of having to pester FCUG to mail me parts a bit at a time. What I'm going to do with them, I'm not too sure. I know that loading them up and giving them away at CommVEx isn't a good idea since I am limited on space in the car. Ebay is an option, but even then by watching some of the sellers with their Commodore wares not moving, it's not too good. JiffyDOS may help, but even that makes it difficult to sell. Most buyers won't know what JiffyDOS is and I can understand that; but for now all I know is that someone is going to have a Merry Christmas other than me and the church will have a copy of the system that I use to write my puppet skits on. Awesome!

Shift-Clr/Home

TITLE: Commodore Therapy

POINT OF ORIGIN: The Interface newsletter

MODE: Commentary

SYNOPSIS: Lenard gives a confessional on how the Commodore computer, its users, and his readers, help him cope with his lifelong battle with bipolarism.

Shift-Clr/Home

Commodore Therapy

Usually and for the most part I am on time with most of the things I plan to do throughout the week and month, but when that stinking disorder that lives within my head decides to flare up, I start falling behind. I start letting both regular as well as important things fall behind to a point where services are threatened to be disconnected and I have to fight through the disorder and get things done. Once in a while a friend or family member will step in and help me play catch up and, for a while, I will do fine, but if this disorder is still running its course through my head, I fall behind again within the next few weeks. I hate the thing, but it is a part of me, and the doctors say there is no cure for it, but it can be managed with proper medication and therapy, and since the disorder is hereditary, I'm afraid that I have spread it on to both of my sons. Maybe somewhere down the line either the medical field will find a cure for this disorder or some future family member will have it bred out of the family line. In either case, it leaves me behind on what is important, for both myself and the Fresno Commodore Users Group.

My name is Lenard and I suffer from bipolar disorder.

Basically, there is a good trade off with this thing: Because of it I am a lot more creative than most of my counterparts with limited imagination. I can usually stare at a blank screen or piece of paper and within just a few short minutes begin to fill same with text of some crazy adventures with little to no effort on my part. Thus, I started chronicling my writings and save them to either Commodore disk, hard drive, or flash drive. I've even become brave and send my writings off to publishers for possible print in a future magazine or book, and many times I have found my name on the masthead of some article in a publication. This is a great feeling to see my work making it out into the public arena even when I'm just doing it because the mental exercise is good for me.

I've come across a few folk who write or draw, and have pages upon pages of material saved to a hard drive or in a drawer somewhere, but they never see the light of publication. When asked, "Why?" most of those I quizzed are afraid of the critic's pen; others fear unwanted exposure; and still others fear that what they have done is not "good enough" for the printing press. To all of them, and I speak as one who thought in all these ways before: It is cow cookies! I have never had so much fun in the game of writing than dealing with critics, dealing with people who enjoy (or hate) my work, and dealing with my own inner demons as to where my work is not "good enough."

What got me to this point was the faithful people who own and use Commodore computers.

When I was asked to do a feature on my BBS back in 1995, I sat down at my Commodore 64 with Speedscript 3.0 booted and went nuts writing and writing about every feature available on my BBS. The article must have taken about five to six pages out of the Commodore Users Group of Kansas City's newsletter and it was a big hit, especially since our newsletter was in trade with several Commodore groups across the country. Gee, I thought this article was only going to go out to the fifteen or so members of the CUGKC. Boy, what a response! Notes were coming in from all over the US and Canada saying how much the readers enjoyed my style of writing. In case you were wondering, yes, this all went to my head! From there on after came a series of articles based on anything I could think of that would tie into the Commodore line of computing. Maybe FCUG has some of these articles in their original format somewhere in the newsletter swap archives. If not, you can find a majority of them reprinted in my collage of a book entitled "Run/Stop-Restore: 10th Anniversary Edition." The article about my BBS is not included in the book, however, so unless the article is preserved somewhere, I don't think a copy will exist, but I can check around in my old CUGKC files and see if I can find it.

But I'm getting off track here... another trap of my condition.

With the CUGKC still asking me for more material from my warped mind about using the Commodore and programming (I published "Check It Out" in 1992), it wasn't long before I was being printed in other magazines, but guess what? That d*mn disorder kicked in and I went into a seemingly ten year hiatus right after the release of the original "Run/Stop-Restore." I wrote very little between 2000 and 2010 until the Fresno Commodore Users Group got me re-interested in Commodore writing. Please understand, between 2000 and 2010 the CUGKC failed; my own attempt to start a Commodore newsletter failed ("The Secret Organization of Commodore Users"); my first book failed; and my marriage failed. It was a tough decade. You may say, "With all that happening, I'd get depressed, too." Thank you, but with bipolar disorder, the depression is due to a lack of serotonin in the brain and does not necessarily need an event to trigger it. My pills balance the mood and fight the depression, but little else. These events just added to the battle. Sometimes you just don't want to fight anymore and death looks like a logical way out. I know from several attempts at suicide that death is not the way out; combating your emotional attitude is the best defense.

Believe it or not, Commodore was a great friend during those moments of depression. The members of FCUG have been very understanding and they always check on me via email to make sure I am doing okay. The doctors have been trying to keep me working at the jobs and the computer to keep me from losing too much serotonin. I also need to exercise daily because work and exercise builds serotonin. This could explain why I feel like poop in the mornings but do better in the afternoons, then to work at either night job (the convenience store or the cleaning job) in the evenings, then do a little typing on the Commodore to wind down before bed keeps the semi-fat man in a balance, but this last round of depression kept me down for the month of August and I've been playing catch up ever since, and now the holidays are fast approaching! What a way to close out 2014!

But again, thank God for Commodore! Whenever a funk grabs me I know that I can go to the Commodore 128 sitting in my computer room and boot a piece of software that will be entertaining or challenge my mind. With both "Commodore Free" and "Reset" magazines kind enough to accept some of my writings I know that my copy of GeoWrite will always be getting some sort of workout as I try to come up with something for either magazine. I've told my doctors about my work and many of them like to read what I have put down on paper.

Please understand that my writings don't just stay with Commodore. I have one book of skits available on Amazon that I am making sales on; I have another skit book ready for publication; and I have a third skit book going through the editing process. I also have flashes of insight that just won't wait too long for me to sit down at the C128 and start typing. I was told by writing teachers that if you can crank out ten pages in two hours then you have hit the apex of a writing groove. I look forward to those days, but don't think that this little rule applies to Commodore programming. As a software programmer I can tell you that if you can get down about one hundred lines of code that are without bugs or need of updating in two hours then you've hit an apex.

So to sum up everything that I've rattled on about in print, let me just say that in order to beat "the blues" whether they be a disorder or just something that comes upon every person now and then, let it be known that sitting down at a great machine like the Commodore is a healthy way to break down the barriers and give you a lift in the areas needed in your emotional life. My son has asked me several times to tear down my Commodore and put it away, but there it sits in the computer room always waiting and always ready to help me fight another injustice of evil as, now and forever, I will be in combat with this thing called bipolarism.

However, let me conclude by giving my apologies to you as a reader of "The Interface" for having the last few issues coming out late. This falls completely on my back and, since I am a big boy, I can take it. I am hoping that I will have my stuff in order by the end of the year. But don't feel like the Lone Ranger in this, reader. I'm a year behind on books and a year behind on plays that I have promised to groups that have almost given up on me. I need to burn out another Commodore keyboard and get these things done.

Shift-Clr/Home

TITLE: Come Sit Right Back And You'll Hear A Tale ....

POINT OF ORIGIN: The Interface newsletter

MODE: Descriptive Narrative

SYNOPSIS: In a desperate attempt to fill space in The Interface, Lenard gives a detailed description of his Commodore desk and set up. Though planned to be an obvious flop of a story, the narrative turned out to be one of the top stories of that year. Read on and find out why.

Shift-Clr/Home

Come Sit Right Back And You'll Hear A Tale

To begin this piece, I would like to ask everyone who reads this and still own and/or uses a Commodore computer to think about writing an article about what their Commodore looks like, how many drives you use and what kind(s), the style of monitor used for video display, any other peripherals you use, and where in your home/office/club it sits. To start the series, let me tell you about my personal Commodore machine...

In a spare bedroom on the south wall of The Roach Center For BASIC Commodore Studies sits my Commodore 128 computer on one of those prefabricated computer stands that you get from Walmart. Back in the day (the desk is about 15 years old) the desk ran for $99.99. I remember putting this unit together with my youngest son. He got to handle the hammer and screw driver and send the nails and screws into the unit, but not until I have hammered the nail half way in and screwed the screw half way in; Calibur got to finish it off and tighten everything down. This desk has a pull out drawer in front where the keyboard sits. This desk also has three cabinets and one file drawer built in; everything is filled with various Commodore disk files, paperwork, and other Commodore projects. This desk is also where I do my paying of bills since I use various Commodore programs to help me keep tally on what I spend, where it went, and how much is left in my check book; another program keeps track on how much I owe on each bill and when it is due next and how much is due upon the next payment. I also use a program that prints on the face of an envelope what I need so I can mail the check off. As for the check itself, I'm still making adjustments to the check printing program so it will work on my new printer I got from FCUG. The printer works great, but with each printer comes new margins, font settings, and other adjustments. I have to get into the check writing program and make PRINT #3 changes by either adding or deleting PRINT #3 statements. This is a long and tedious process

221

and is best to do when you have actual checks to write, otherwise you'll be wasting checks in order to make your check print perfect. With each PRINT #3 adjustment I save and try to print again. Big fun and good times.

On the left lower side of the desk is a door that is suppose to hold one of those old tower hard drives that stood about three feet tall. RJ came up with the idea of adding boards and supports for those boards so I could put all three of my drives – a 1541, a 1571, and a 1581 – into that space. This worked real well except of dealing with all the cables and cords that come with activating and using these drives. After building the shelves, RJ started developing in his mind an idea of making a Commodore disk tower that would have all three disk drives built in and the ability to change the disk drive's designation on the front of the unit by a simple push of a button. Unfortunately, before RJ could start on the project, someone on Homestead built this very same thing and was offering it over the Internet for a nominal price. I never got this unit on Homestead since at the time it would be an insult and a slap in the face to my son, so in the desk is the three tier shelving unit he built to hold each one of my Commodore drives.

On the desk itself, well, we might call it a mess. Papers are strewn everywhere. As a writer, I have lots of projects started and never finished, projects that I have yet to find a publisher for, and ideas that need to be expanded into a full size stories or articles. If those who read this remember when I brought an uninterruptible power source to be auctioned off for the CommVEx, I have one of these units running my entire Commodore set up A flick of one switch and my entire Commodore set up is booted. This UPS unit has saved my Commodore work several times during severe weather here in Kansas. All these units are designed to is give you enough time to finish your work and save to disk. Most units that are small have about fifteen minutes of power; bigger units can go as long as four to eight hours. We have a big unit that takes two motorcycle size batteries that is used to run our router, one more to run any desktops, and one running the Mac Mini found in the office. As you can probably guess, we love our computers and other electronic gaming devices.

On the top of the desk to the left is where the Commodore 1902 monitor resides. Underneath it is one of those selective power strips so a user doesn't have to bend down and switch off devices individually; just toggle one of the switches to turn off that particular device. It is very handy when you are fat like me and can't bend over like I used to.

This particular desk comes with a cabinet on the right that is under lock and key for those items you wish no one else to get in their possession. I'm sure this was designed to put in things like OS disks and other boot programs that a user spends hundreds of dollars to procure. I leave the door unlocked because I want anyone who sits at the Commodore to use what I have. Here is where I keep my GEOS and other word processing packages so I won't have to search my disk files to find.

Two shelves occupy the center rear of the desk where I keep programs that I am currently using or creating. The bottom shelf is separated into four pockets that I keep my small Commodore tools in or disks I plan to use soon. One pocket is just the right size to hold a 3.5" disk file comfortably. These 3.5's I use to transfer information between my PC and the Commodore and back again, if necessary. The file also contains everything I am looking for in the way of anything to use on my 1581 disk drive. The top shelf usually contains items like a disk notcher for the 5.25" disks and other Commodore related items.

Now, to finish the tour of my desk off, we get to the very top where the Star NX1000-C printer resides along with two stereo speakers for good sound coming from the Commodore's SID chip. The printers have changed over the years as I use more and more Commodore printing programs. When I had my first Commodore 64 and I was working as a custodian for a major department store chain here in the metro, I was the pimp of computers. If anyone needed something printed off or a program to do a certain thing, I was the "go to" guy. I made plenty of banners to announce upcoming special events and found programs that would help those who needed special things done that, at the time, only Commodore could do. I even made videos for the Junior's Department that showed me playing games (and losing) or creating music videos using Swinth or other music displaying programs. These were popular among the teen crowd at the time and would create a draw to that department, which meant sales for the area. Commodore was king to the entire store and they loved it when I came up with another program or video to help the store along. I didn't get paid extra for this but it was fun to do and getting to use the Commodore any day of the week was awesome.

And please, don't let me forget the most important item of my Commodore set up other than the Commodore itself, and that is "The Commodore Cat," Hennessy. He was a "throw away" cat that someone begged me to take in and care for. It took him a while to adjust to my other three cats that already occupy most of the space in the Roach Center, but everyone got to deal with him and give him the proper respect that is due each animal here. Hennessy is a "tuxedo" tabby with white "boots" and a large white "emblem" on his chest and underside. Hennessy would, when I am working on the Commodore, jump onto the desk, prance around with what little space was available, and lay down right smack dab in the middle of the desk, usually on some work I was doing, whether it be disks that I am using or papers I am working on, demanding that I spend a couple of moments with him. I used to take him off the desk and go back to my work, but he would jump back up and take the same spot he formerly occupied. Over the couple of years that Hennessy has been here, we have worked out a compromise where he gets to lay down anywhere he wants on the desk, and I throw whatever work I am doing on top of him. He doesn't mind this; he just stretches out, purrs, and lets me do my thing. This could be why I have so many disks that no longer load into the Commodore's memory; the static electricity stored in Hennessy's fur is causing data corruption on the disk and thus failure to load. I've lost plenty of data this way, but I am learning that, when I have done a major work, like the Five Pack Bonus Disk I'm working on for the upcoming CommVEx, I make a second copy and put it away – far away from Hennessy.

So, that is the boring and tedious set up where I have my Commodore make home. Of course, the entire room is strewn with Commodore computers and other Commodore related items that have yet to find permanent homes. Most of these units will be donated to the local Goodwill; other non-functioning machines will be stripped of chips and set out onto the curb for recycling. Out of all this Commodore equipment, I don't have one SuperCPU or other Commodore related accelerators; just stock Commodore units.

Shift-Clr/Home

Shift-Clr/Home

www.ingramcontent.com/pod-product-compliance
Lightning Source LLC
Chambersburg PA
CBHW071113050326
40690CB00008B/1206